CAREER PROJECTION 101

An Independent Contractor's

GUIDE

to a Successful Business and Balanced Life

Clem Harrod

CLEMCO.U
Tampa, FL

Copyright © 2020 by Clementé Linwood Philip Harrod

All rights reserved. No part of this publication may be reproduced, distributed, or transmitted in any form or by any means, including photocopying, recording, or other electronic or mechanical methods, without the prior written permission of the publisher, except in the case of brief quotations embodied in critical reviews and certain other noncommercial uses permitted by copyright law. For permission requests, write to the publisher, addressed "Attention: Permissions Coordinator," via this website: www.clemcou.com | @clemcoav

Ordering Information:

    Quantity sales. Special discounts are available on quantity purchases by schools, corporations, associations, and others. For details, contact the publisher at www.clemcou.com. Orders by U.S. trade bookstores and wholesalers. Please contact: CLEMCO.U at www.clemcou.com.

Printed in the United States of America

This publication is designed to provide competent and reliable information regarding the subject matter covered. However, it is sold with the understanding that the author and publisher are not engaged in rendering legal, financial, or other professional advice. Laws and practices often vary from state to state and if legal or other expert assistance is required, the services of a professional should be sought. The author and publisher specifically disclaim any liability incurred from the use or application of the contents of this book.

Events, locales and conversations have been recreated from the author's best memories of them. In some instances, to maintain the anonymity of individuals mentioned in this publication, the author has changed names, places, identifying characteristics and details such as physical properties, occupations and places of residence.

First Printing: 2020

ISBN: 978-1-7347452-9-0

Cover design by CCS Marketing

Cover grid by Scott Flanagan

Smooth Projectionist photograph by Bruce Couch

Smooth Projectionist logo by James Leslie

Author back cover headshot photograph by Trevor Collinson

Author "About the Author" photograph by Donovan Muir

Interior photographs by Lynnette Wisk, Chris "Chiili" Horton, Gary Bassing, Kelly Foxen, Toriano Evans, Greg Wilson, and Reginald Duncan

Storyboard illustrations by MasterCharlie (www.fiverr.com)

Interior formatting by Crystal Crawford

"To the youths who march onward and upward toward the light, this volume is respectively dedicated."

—Charles H. Wesley

"For generational knowledge and understanding is one of the most powerful things in the world. However, the lack thereof is one of the deadliest."

—Clem Harrod

To an industry who understood me when I felt misunderstood, valued me when I felt devalued, and accepted me when I felt unacceptable.

You saw me before I saw myself, and I always felt appreciated when I was with you. You helped me find my way out of poverty and discover a life I never dreamed I could have. You were my first love, and I will forever be grateful.

Thank you!

Contents

Foreword..7
Introduction...9
Act I: The Walk-In...11

Chapter 1:
How Do I Get Started?..19

Chapter 2:
How Do I Get New Clients?......................................35

Chapter 3:
How Do I Find a Specialty?......................................55

Chapter 4:
How Do I Build New & Maintain Old Relationships?..............73

Act II: The Show..89

Chapter 5:
How Do I Set Up a Budget?.......................................97

Chapter 6:
How Do I Decide on a Business Model?..........................117

Chapter 7:
How Do I Get Insurance?..135

Chapter 8:
How Do I Plan for My Financial Future?........................153

Act III: The Walk-Out..165

Chapter 9:
How Do I Retire?..173

About CLEMCO.HR	188
About CLEMCO.AV	190
About the Author	191
Photos	191
Acknowledgments	200

Foreword

Having worked in the corporate meeting world for nearly forty years as a Professional Technical Director, I have had the great good fortune to meet some very impressive people whose approach to work and life has colored our industry profoundly. In this book, Clem Harrod solidifies his position at the top of that list. This step-by-step guide to building a successful career by putting the all-important intangible skills first makes this book a must-read for anyone considering a career in corporate theatre.

By focusing less on the tangible skills related to actually creating perfect pictures on screen using projectors, Clem focuses instead on what it takes to find work, build nurturing relationships and creating your personal brand. These bedrock concepts are seldom, if ever, taught in our university classes, making this book indispensable for professionals at every level of our industry. Nearly everyone I run into these days has made a transition from one type of employment model to another. Employee to freelance, freelance to small company, and everything in between. A common thread in these transitions is that everyone needs help with the day-to-day issues of insurance, accounting, compliance and how to find the right people to guide us effectively. In *Career Projection 101*, Clem provides a no-nonsense road map to addressing these issues and provides the resources to get it done.

Perhaps the most engaging theme in this book is how important it is to use the skills and experience we have accumulated to help lift the next generation of professionals to reach their best lives, both personally and professionally. In this regard, Clem is the master, providing countless examples of how he has used every experience to make himself the best husband, father and event professional he can be. These examples can be put to work immediately in our lives and finding so many in one book is Clem's gift to us.

When Clem first shared this book with me, I read it immediately and was actually surprised at how much information was pertinent to my personal situation. I have reread this book several times and am now working with the business accountant that CLEMCO has used for years. I have a deep respect for Clem and what he brings to the issue of personal ethics. *Career Projection 101* gives us all important insight into how we create our professional legacy through hard work and dedication to becoming the best version of our personal selves. Congratulations to all of you that have added this important book to your personal libraries.

Tom Bollard
Husband, Father, Technical Director (in that order…)
Live Event Production/Corporate Theater

Introduction

The purpose of this book is to help Independent Contractors, Freelancers, and Small Business Owners better manage their time, money, and relationships by answering the questions,

"How do I..."

- Get Started
- Get Noticed
- Find a Specialty

all the way to:

- Create a Budget
- Find an Accountant
- Get Health Insurance

and ultimately:

- How Do I Retire

Written in an act format—Act I: The Walk-In, Act II: The Show, and Act III: The Walk-Out—*Career Projection 101* will become a prerequisite for anyone starting a career and life in the Live Event Production Industry.

I understand the challenges I faced trying to figure out how to best manage a 1099 lifestyle. This book is the culmination of all I have learned as I built my business from the ground up.

Television Production has been a part of my life since middle school. Its influence, in addition to my church, home, school, family and friends, has led to this moment in time—this moment of my destiny—to share this story with you. These are my struggles and my victories bound together to help you understand your life, your destiny, and how to achieve the projected image you see for yourself.

Projected image, you say? *What is that?*

Inside all of us is a light. A source. A ray of hope. I believe that light wants to come out. That light wants to shine. That light of greatness is what the world needs and wants to see. For me, that light is this book.

When I entered into my career, I had no plan, no path, no model image to follow. The way had not yet been paved. No one had gone from start to finish and then come back to show or tell us how to make a living as an Independent Contractor in the Live Event Production Industry. I pray this book is your path. I pray this book shows you how to Walk In your industry, execute the Show of your career, and Walk Out when your mind and body are tired and ready to move on.

A Walk-Out occurred once in my career when I left the sports broadcasting sector of the industry. I was ill prepared for that moment, and I quickly had to learn how to adapt and change. Now that my focus is solely on another sector of my industry, I will be ready when my time for retirement comes.

This book is my journey as I achieve the success I'm destined for, and the success I hope you achieve as well. Enjoy!

#Projection101

Act I:
The Walk-In

The journey begins as you walk into the industry, uncertain of your path or what the future will hold.

FADE IN:

INT: GAYLORD PALMS, OSCEOLA BALLROOM, ORLANDO, FL. DAY

It is February 2002, and CLEM, a young, twenty-two-year-old college graduate, arrives at his first corporate event. CLEM was hired by a well-known local rental and staging company to help strike, or tear down, one of Ernst & Young's large partner conventions. CLEM enters the ballroom anxious and terrified but in awe of the amount of activity underway. In spite of being nervous, CLEM attempts to look like he has it all together.

CLEM walks towards the Video Department in search of MARK, his point of contact. With a wet and clammy hand, CLEM greets MARK, ready for his first task.

          CLEM:
Hi! Where should I get started?

          MARK:
You can go over there and start wrapping.

CLEM starts wrapping cables and struggles to put them away in the right cases. MARK takes one look at CLEM'S work and shakes his head in disgust.

> MARK:
> Let's hurry up. Get these cables wrapped and put away in their cases. No, not that case. The other case.

> CLEM:
> (flustered and stammering) This one?

> MARK:
> No! The other one! (with a snarky attitude) Geez, didn't they teach you anything in school?

MARK says this sarcastically, but CLEM is unaware of MARK's sense of humor, and takes it personally.

> MARK:
> We need to hurry up and strike this set. I've got a flight out in the morning.

CLEM tries again, wrapping the cable over under and under over. It ends up in a perfect loop. CLEM looks up, hoping MARK will approve. Instead, he glares.

> MARK:
> Don't just stand there! Get the next one!

CLEM hurries to the next cable, terrified he has screwed up his first real job, and wonders if this is a career he should pursue.

1. CLEM enters the ballroom anxious and terrified, but in awe of the amount of activity underway.

2. With a wet and clammy hand, CLEM greets MARK ready for his first task.

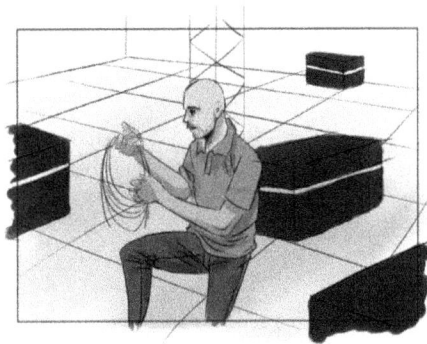

3. CLEM starts wrapping cables and struggles to get them put away in the right cases.

4. MARK takes one look at CLEM'S work and gives him a look of disgust.

5. No! The other one!

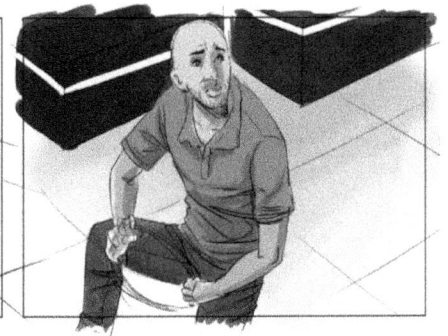

6. CLEM looks up, hoping MARK will approve.

Chapter 1: How Do I Get Started?

That happened the first day at my first corporate event. I had just graduated from Florida State and had plenty of experience working in sports. But this was an entirely different world and an opportunity I didn't want to mess up.

All my life, I've enjoyed telling stories through video and still images, but my interest really sparked when I started taking Television Production classes in middle school. I even went to a special high school where I studied the subject for two out of my six classes each year. I was an active volunteer in my church's Communications Department, and I worked on some of the first episodes of their broadcasted show, *Right Connection*. Upon graduation, I was fortunate enough to attend Florida State University and enroll in the Media Production program. There I had access to some of the best equipment money could buy, but it was my experience in the Seminole Productions classes that truly opened my eyes to the opportunities that life had to offer.

Career Projection 101

You see, I had grown up in poverty, the only child of a single mom, and had spent some time homeless. I often reflect on the night we slept in our car under the lights of the iconic Hollywood water tower in South Florida. It's a reminder of how far I've come, and how determined and blessed I am. Everything I wanted, I had to work harder than the next kid to receive, and this job—my first real job—was no exception.

Be Where They Need You to Be

After college, I applied for every available internship all over the country. Finally hearing back from one, I felt honored when Rick Price asked me to join his team at the Orlando Magic. There was a sense of home and family within the organization and I loved the people with whom I worked. I didn't want that feeling to end. I knew the only way to turn that internship into a full-time job was to have a strong work ethic and show myself worthy. That was something I learned early on from my mom and it was reinforced when I pledged my fraternity.

During our process, we memorized a quote that I still use today to guide my decisions and actions: "A task once begun, never leave it 'til it's done. Be the labor great or small, do it well or not at all."

For every task Rick or Jason Dewberry, my other supervisor, asked of me, I tried to go above and beyond. I felt like that was what I was supposed to do. It was my duty. *How can I be of assistance? What can I do to help?*

How Do I Get Started?

I constantly tried to anticipate where I needed to be and how I could help. I didn't have much experience in certain areas, but I had an eagerness and a willingness to learn and please. That mindset had gotten me that far in life, so something about my approach had to be right.

Steve Uhlmer, a former Orlando Magic intern, was not only a Camera Operator who worked the game night broadcast, he was also a Camera Operator on the convention side of the industry. Steve saw that eagerness in me when I served as his Camera Utility and decided to give me a shot at a new opportunity. Maybe Steve saw something in me that reminded him of himself, or something he wanted more of in the industry. Either way, Steve made a phone call, put his reputation on the line, and got me on the call list that brought me to my first real corporate production event. Every time I see Steve, I thank him for taking a risk on a tall, awkward kid from Miami, FL.

> **C.L.E.M. Note**
>
> **Be willing to serve.**
>
> This is a service-based industry and you must be willing and have the heart to serve, regardless of whether you are a Stagehand or a company owner. Like Tom Kervitsky and Mike Compton of TEK Productions, you can wrap a cable—even if you're the one wearing a suit.

That's the key to getting started: being in the right place at the right time. Whether you are volunteering or working an event, try to anticipate what the people you are working with will need and want. From an extra battery to a bottle of water, if you place their needs above your own, they will think about you and remember your name when the time is right.

Be Willing to Step Outside of Your Comfort Zone

I thought I knew what I was doing when I agreed to work that convention. After all, when I was in college, and later while working as an intern, I had done video shoots for player interviews, press conferences, media events, game day shoots, as well as setting up our studio for coaches' shows and going out to community events with the players. I even had the opportunity to travel on the Orlando Magic team plane for a baseball game FSU played against the Miami Hurricanes. I knew how to pack up the gear, making sure we had everything, and then set up the equipment with ease. However, the corporate world was an entirely different ball game.

First of all, the events were massive. There was audio, video, rigging, scenic, staging, and lighting, with hundreds of people working together to build and execute a multimedia show. I felt like every second of every show was run-run-run, go-go-go. There was no room or time to rethink or hesitate. The professionals around me relied on my ability to know what, how, and when to do everything expected of me.

I was floundering in deep waters and I had a choice—sink or swim. I chose to swim, even though I was unsure and afraid to make a mistake. When I needed help, I asked for it. When I needed to improvise a solution, I came up with one. That's not to say I never messed up, but my eagerness to learn and work hard helped propel me in the industry.

How Do I Get Started?

I often found myself working with people who had plans in their heads and knew how they wanted them executed, but didn't share all the details. Or they expected me to read their minds and know what to do. If you find yourself in these types of situations, ask questions, take notes, and ask for help if needed. You may stumble and fall, but if you are eager to serve, present, show up and work hard, you will succeed. Don't be on your phone, hiding in the corner, or taking long breaks, because that is a surefire way to be noticed for the wrong reasons. You're part of a team—and that means being there, supporting your brother or sister and fulfilling your role.

Maybe you're nervous, anxious or insecure about the part you play in all of this. I remember that feeling: stepping into a new role, a new ballroom, unsure of how to move forward or what to do. It was years ago for me, but this might be you, today. Still not sure if this is the career you want, or maybe you're stuck on the sidelines, wanting this job but unsure how to break into the Live Event Production Industry (or any industry, for that matter). If this is you, don't give up!

The Perfect Shot

I recently crewed an event in Sarasota, FL with thirteen Stagehands. It was pouring rain, cold, and we had to strike an outdoor set in the mud.

As Steve Uhlmer did for me, I offered someone I didn't know that well a position on the team. He drove two hours to the location (with no travel pay or lodging), spent all those hours in the rain and cold with us, and then drove home in the middle of the night. He was prepared with rain gear and had a great attitude. He worked hard and proved his worth.

He was my first call when I needed to fill another position a week later.

Make it Happen

Jobs don't just come to you. They won't fall in your lap out of thin air. No one's going to show up at your door and offer to train you and give you a shot. *You have to make it happen.*

For thirteen years, I drove between Tampa and Orlando to work Orlando Magic games. I received a small mileage allowance, but no one paid for a hotel room. I stayed with friends and often slept in my car at the rest stop just outside of Lakeland. I paid my dues because I was focused on the bigger picture, not the small one in my camera lens.

You have to be willing to volunteer and give up your time to find out what interests you and what you love to do. The Production Industry has so many facets: news, sports, corporate conventions, concerts and touring, Broadway shows, etc. All of these are live events and require some form of production. They also require a slightly different skill set and knowledge base. I spent time working in almost all of these areas, and because of that varied experience, I realized you don't truly know your passion until you try things out.

When I interned for the Magic, I averaged sixty hours a week and made $211.76 *every two weeks*. That didn't even cover my portion of the rent. I had to take out a student loan in order to support myself, but I didn't care. I understood what I had to do, and I knew I had an opportunity that was going to lead to something big. When you're presented with your opportunity, your moment, take it! You have to do what you have to do to get where you want to go.

Show Up Like a Professional

There's an old saying, "Dress for the job you want, instead of the one you have." I'd take that a step further and advise to have the mindset of the job you want and not the one you have. Study the people who are where you want to be, then act and dress accordingly. Understand how they achieved their success and envision yourself there as well. That starts with analyzing and examining your actions and asking yourself, "Is this my best? Am I projecting the best image possible?"

Remember, you aren't just representing yourself. You're representing your employer, as well as their client. If you don't fit the mold they need or want and you're not willing to adjust or change, they will replace you. That's how my industry works—there are *always* redundancies. If one machine goes down, we can fill the void with another. There are people waiting to fill your spot as well. Think of them as redundancies waiting and eager to do the job. They will learn from your mistakes and take any opportunities you miss if you aren't ready and willing to do whatever it takes.

This is something that is always on my mind and that's why I am always looking to represent my End Client to the best of my ability. In my case, my End Client is God. He is my source of strength and the reason I do what I do. That shows in what I wear, how I speak to people, how I carry myself, and how I do my work.

I realized a few key principles early in my career that led to my success. If you want to consistently work in your industry, you should consider adopting them as well:
- Be present and attentive
- Dress neatly and professionally
- Have a good attitude
- Be flexible
- Be willing to learn
- Be humble

After embodying and living by these virtues, measure your growth and see how far you've come. That's the true definition of Projection101.

FLASHBACK

At any event, there are usually two projectors per screen: a main projector and a backup for redundancy. The two images have to be converged, or overlapped, with a grid so that whatever is coming out of the backup projector fits perfectly on top of the image from the primary projector.

In 2008, I was a young Audio-Visual Technician, hired as a Video Projectionist, and working an event at the Caribe Royale in Orlando. New to the role and unprepared for the job, I didn't know how to make my grids overlap perfectly. My image was extremely blurry and instead of finding out what to do and asking for help, I turned on one projector and shuttered the other. The owner of the rental and staging company, who happened to be on-site that day, came up to me and asked why both projectors weren't on. There was only one answer, and he already knew it. I had to admit my mistake and ask for help. I didn't defend my work or come up with an excuse. I sought assistance and listened as directions were given.

The person I turned to for help was Mark—the same tech from my first day on the job. He was there working the show, and I felt he was the best person to guide me through the projection conversion process. Mark not only supported me in that moment, but also taught me techniques I still use to this day.

Humbling yourself before a person with the authority and experience will not change a mistake, but it will show you as a person willing to own your choices and learn from them.

FADE IN:

INT: PEABODY HOTEL (NOW HYATT REGENCY). ORLANDO, FL. DAY

It is 2011, and CLEM has been working as a sports, corporate event, and local news Camera Operator for several years. These opportunities have led him to shooting NBA Finals, NBA All-Star Games, NHL's Stanley Cup, and several MLB, NFL and collegiate sporting events. Though he is consistently working in those sectors of the industry, CLEM's desire is to accept more corporate event jobs, and take on the role of a Video Projectionist. He has the knowledge and understanding of the position, just not the frequency to truly excel.

CLEM is backstage working an event and is trying to muster up the courage to ask the client about moving into a bigger role. Nervous and anxious, CLEM rehearses what he'll say to KARI, the corporate event client/producer. Trying to keep his voice steady, CLEM approaches KARI as she stands near his handheld camera and the 9'x16' rear projection screen.

KARI:
Hi Clem! You are doing such a great job. Thank you so much.

CLEM:
No problem. I am happy to be here. Thank *you* for having me!

KARI:
(with a smile on her face) Certainly! Thank *you* for being here.

CLEM:
(nervous and struggling not to show it, CLEM asks) Kari, do you have a moment to talk?

KARI:
Sure! What's up?

CLEM:
(stammering a bit) Well, (long pause) I appreciate the opportunity you have given me to serve as a Camera Operator on your events... You know my work ethic and my desire to tell a good story through the camera lens. But, (another long pause) I really want to try something else. I really want to

> move into Video Projection. I have been working as a Projectionist for my other clients and I'd like to do this with you all as well.

KARI, not expecting this conversation, thinks about CLEM's request. She has been impressed with CLEM thus far but is hesitant to trust him with this additional responsibility. Furthermore, KARI is afraid to lose CLEM as a Camera Operator because of his experience and what he brings to a production.

CLEM is scared to be rejected, but knows if he doesn't take this shot, he may never move up to where he wants to be.

> CLEM:
> Kari, I can see you are a little reluctant. I want to assure you that I will work as hard as I always have, and I will continue to be dedicated to your events. I may not get things right every time, but I will learn from my mistakes and improve upon them.

                    KARI:
(still contemplating her thoughts, KARI makes a decision) All right. We'll put you on the list for one of our upcoming shows. But Clem . . .

                    CLEM:
Yes?

                    KARI:
Think of this like a first date. It doesn't have to be perfect, but it does have to be good enough for us to bring you back for a second one.

CLEM nods and hurries back to his camera in anticipation of the show's Walk-In. He's excited to have this chance and is determined not to mess it up.

1. CLEM is backstage working an event.

2. Nervous and anxious, CLEM rehearses what he'll say to KARI.

3. I really want to try something else. I really want to move into video projection.

4. KARI, not expecting this conversation, thinks about CLEM's request.

5. It doesn't have to be perfect, but it does have to be good enough for us to bring you back for a second one.

6. He's excited to have this chance, and is determined not to mess it up.

Chapter 2

How Do I Get New Clients?

When I first started in this industry, I wasn't quite sure what I wanted to do. I was a fairly decent Camera Op from my time in church, high school, and college, but my skills really began to develop during my internship, or what I like to call "Grad School," with the Magic. I learned all the tips and tricks and gained much-needed professional experience. Unfortunately, I wasn't making enough money.

Derek Fuchs, a coworker from the Magic, recommended me for a job at the NBC affiliate, WESH in Orlando. After working there for a year, I moved to Tampa and worked for the FOX affiliate, WTVT. Relocating across the state meant working long hours with long commutes between the two cities. Taking gigs at one-off sporting events made for extremely long days/nights, but the more I worked on the convention side of the business, the more I wanted to be a part of their multi-day shows. The positions I filled at these events consisted of Stagehand, AV

Tech and Camera Op roles, but my interest began leaning towards Video Projection.

I soon realized if I wanted those jobs, I needed to take the opportunities to increase my experience and gradually build my confidence and faith in my abilities. When I reached that point of assuredness in 2011, my friend Robert Permenter encouraged me to talk to my client and ask if I could become a part of their production team. That conversation with Kari led to new opportunities and, eventually, the business I have today.

For those of you who are new to this industry, trying to move into a different sector, interested in a different role on the crew, or who want to build a business and clientele from scratch, seek out and have those difficult conversations. That is the only way to make those connections. It's a lot like dating. From finding out where the potential matches are, to connecting, to settling down—if you don't take the risk, you may never find your mate.

> **C.L.E.M. Note**
>
> **Create and maintain an environment that is attractive to clients.**
>
> No matter how stressful a job gets, I try to maintain a positive, uplifting attitude. Things can, and often do, go wrong, but that *we've got it under control* attitude can make a big difference.
>
> You never know who is watching and observing your demeanor. If you show yourself as willing to assist and resolve an issue, you also show yourself as a team player. Many of my team's job opportunities have come from clients who liked our work ethic and attitude to help.

Set Up Your Parameters

When you join a dating site to find a potential mate, you check off boxes and provide information that specifies your age range, location, and interests. These details help narrow down the vast number of candidates into something that more accurately fits your lifestyle and what you're looking for. It's much the same when building your client list.

Start by:

>**Defining your brand:** Before you make that first call to obtain work from a client, know your brand. Essentially, know what you stand for. Know how you want people to feel about you and respond when they hear your name. This is a powerful, proactive process to build your reputation. There's a line in the play *Hamilton* where Alexander says, "If you stand for nothing, Burr, what'll you fall for?" That's my attitude about business—you should stand for something. People should know you have values and you believe in a greater cause. For instance, I wear a black, gray, or blue company logoed shirt every time I work an event. My shirts say either CLEMCO and #Projection101 or Certified AV Technician. CLEMCO is an acronym which means Coach, Lead, Educate and Mentor, while Certified is a part of our brand and lets clients know about our commitment to the success of their event. At a glance, those in the industry know my resume and reputation. The dark, clean-logoed shirt and pants allow me to stand out yet fit in at the same time. You should do the same.

Maybe not with the logoed shirt based on your client's work attire requirements, but with a clean and professional look. Promoting a brand that says *responsible, attentive and hardworking* to a client is an instant attraction and could lead to future opportunities.

Determining your preferred sector/market: Try not to be too narrow with your focus at first. If your ultimate dream is to work NBA games, start with any sport. Whether it is collegiate soccer, spring training baseball, or local high school championship football, it is all experience to make you a more skilled technician. I had no desire to shoot drag car racing in Sarasota, Florida or run cables on the golf course at Innisbrook, but those jobs gave me the experience of working in those environments, with that gear, and with those clients. That's what you're looking for: experience and a reputation of being a great person to work with. To do that, you need to cast a wide net.

Setting your rate: Since you are building your business from the ground up, set a fair market rate. Don't make it too low because people will wonder if you are working so cheaply because it's a reflection of your skill level and quality of work. You also don't want to make your rate too high and price yourself out of your market. Come in somewhere in the middle. If you're unsure about what you should charge, ask yourself: What is my time and expertise worth? You can also ask a fellow contractor who is close to your skill level what they charge. The market will let you know if you are priced appropriately.

Maintaining a positive, can-do attitude: You won't land the big jobs or your desired position right away. You'll need to pay your dues, just like everyone who came before you. When I was a Camera Utility for the Magic, I knew I was capable of shooting the games. However, the opportunities weren't yet available to me. In order to gain more experience and get my hours behind the lens, I would drive almost two hours from Tampa to Orlando, for no additional mileage rate, and shoot high school sporting events for the Orlando Sentinel Varsity Sports Show. Those two-hour games barely paid anything and I drove all over Orange, Seminole, and Volusia counties gathering highlights. It was tiring, hopping from event to event, but my time there was invaluable. I made great connections and continued to hone my craft. After two years of working those high school games, it wasn't long before I shot one of my first Magic Games on Christmas Day in 2003.

Don't be afraid to take the smaller jobs, or even to work for free or at a reduced rate, just to get your foot in the door. Wrap cables, haul equipment, or even get coffee and snacks. All of these tasks, done with a positive attitude, display persistence and dedication. Show that you can do the job—no matter the job—and a client will be much more likely to hire you again.

Get Over the Fear of Rejection

People are going to say *no*. That's a fact. The opposite is also true—there will be some people who say *yes*. Everyone has a fear of rejection, but the people who succeed are the ones who ignore that feeling and press forward. If someone says no, move on—that relationship wasn't meant to be or wasn't meant for that time. When I mentioned my desire to take on more roles as a Video Projectionist to Kari, and then asked for an opportunity to do so, she could have easily said *no*. I had to be prepared for that. Even after speaking to Robert, and knowing he believed in me, there was still a possibility of rejection. I was dealing with a two-sided coin, and I had to be willing to gamble. I had to know that if she didn't see me as a good fit, someone else would. This applies to any job, any position, and any relationship. Be prepared for either answer and always move on with grace and respect. This is a small industry and today's *no* could be tomorrow's *yes*.

Just know you don't have to be the best at everything. No one expects you to be. I certainly am not, a fact I freely admit. Clients aren't hiring me because they expect me to be a master at *every* aspect of my job and this business. They hire me because they want me and what I do have to

---

The Perfect Shot

I was recently an attendee at an event and I noticed the panelists weren't being heard in the back of the room. They had microphones, but the levels needed to be adjusted based on where the microphones were being held. I understood the issue and knew how to fix it.

I tracked down the unattended audio board and made the adjustments to solve the problem. It wasn't my show but that didn't matter. I wanted to help everyone have their best experience and I wanted the organization to look their best as well. That's my attitude no matter where I am—project the best image possible—and I am willing to do my part to help others achieve that.

Unexpectedly, I made a new connection at that luncheon and I anticipate it leading to another client.

offer—the Clem Factor, as I like to call it. They know that I will show up, get the job done, and put my all into every project. They know I will be respectful, polite, grateful, and ready to serve. My clients also know I will use my resources to resolve problems if I don't already have the answer. These traits aren't just a part of my company brand—they are a part of my personal brand and who I am as an individual. These are the parts my clients hire when they bring me onto a project, and these are the parts I am happy to give.

Always Maintain the Relationship

After I complete a job, I make sure to not only thank the client for the work, but also for the opportunity to serve them. I learned that from my good friend and Lighting Designer, Richard Dunn. This is a service-based industry and when you position yourself as a helper and problem solver, people will be more likely to hire you. For me, the service approach is part of my faith. I believe in helping people and meeting whatever needs they have, not just for a paycheck but because I am called to do so.

That being said, I never leave a job on bad terms. Not every client works out and not every job goes well. But if it's your fault, take responsibility and do what you can to fix it. I have encountered difficult clients and felt they were hard to please. Instead of complaining to them or about them, I've tried to figure out how I can best communicate with them. I understand not everyone is able to translate their thoughts and ideas, but it's our responsibility to best serve our End Client. You never know what is going on in a person's life or how those challenges may be affecting their words and actions. Stay calm and keep the end goal in mind. You may work with that person again somewhere down the road and you want all memories to be positive ones. Remember, every bridge you burn is one you can't later cross in the future.

Look for the Five Cs

When ready to settle down and get married, it's customary to purchase a diamond ring for their bride-to-be. Things a jeweler will tell you to consider before you buy are the cut, clarity, color, carat, and cost of the stone. When a client is looking to hire a technician for their event, they are consciously and subconsciously considering similar things. Based on their core values, business model, and mission statement, clients are looking for Independent Contractors who fit their mold.

Instead of the Five Cs, clients typically concentrate on these attributes to determine who they will hire and how much they will pay:

- Technical Ability
- Customer Service/Relationship Management
- Appearance
- Trustworthiness

Disney's Event Production/Event Group was a department that did this exceptionally well. They hired the best clean-cut technicians to operate their attractions, conventions, and corporate events, because they needed people who best represented their brand. As a company, Disney continues to cultivate relationships with its customers by providing superior service, attending to every possible need, and solving any problems that arise. In addition, Disney is famous for its pristine appearance and keeping any issues or problems out of the public's view. As a result, Disney has built a globally recognized and trustworthy brand that is considered a top international destination.

Use the Law of Attraction

I'm sure you are familiar with the saying *opposites attract*. In fact, Paula Abdul sang about it in her 1988 hit bearing the same name. But have you heard the saying *like attracts like*?

According to the Law of Attraction, people operate in tones, rhythms, and frequencies, and constantly exude energy. The pace at which they operate either attracts or repels people and circumstances from their lives. If you believe in this philosophy, think about the energy of the people in your life and the people with whom you surround yourself. What is their character? What is their work ethic? What do people say about their brand?

Now, turn that thought around. What do people say about you, your work ethic, your character, or your brand? Is it attractive? Is it something worthy of the type of clients with whom or type of shows with which you want to work?

Every social media post and interaction, both in person and online, is being analyzed consciously and subconsciously. People have determined whether or not they like you before you hand them a business card or ask to set up a meeting. Your energy says it all. So, I ask you: "What does yours say?" Does your energy say, "I am available and will work hard?" Does it say, "I am technically knowledgeable and a problem solver?" Does it say, "I am a people pleaser and want to help move things forward?" Or, does your energy say, "I am a complainer. I point out people's flaws and don't do anything to help them. I also sit around waiting for others to finish their tasks after I've completed mine"? If it's the former instead of the latter, people will notice that and start booking you for their events. In its simplest form, that's how the Law of Attraction works. You will attract, and be happy with, clients who fit your mold and you theirs. You exude the same frequency of energy and will be drawn to one another to manifest your success.

Keep in Touch

After you've established the relationship and found a client you've enjoyed "dating"—keep in touch. Reach out to them and say hello. As I was working my way up in the industry, I made a point to reach out to people from time to time, just to say hi. Nothing more and nothing less than just hello. That sparked a genuine interest in that person's life and the life of their family members. I truly cared about their wellbeing. Work and opportunities sometimes developed from those conversations, but that was never my intention. I simply reached out when people crossed my mind.

Many of the people on my crew today are there because they did the same with me. They reached out and said hello. They scheduled times through my website, we had conversations, and we got to know one another. I saw they were persistent but not annoying, confident but not cocky, and had a heart to help. I began to see them as people I could trust with my clients. So, when I needed to expand my crew, they were the people I hired.

Through the years, I've realized what you put out in the world comes back to you. If you constantly maintain a positive, can-do attitude, express gratitude, and have a willingness to serve, good things will happen. You can call it karma, the golden rule, or planting a seed. Focus on being your very best, and you will find that building your clientele becomes easier and easier with every job.

How Do I Get New Clients?

FLASHBACK

One of the most important things about acquiring new clients is transitioning between them, or as I like to put it, "The Handoff." People are often very excited about the newness of a relationship and want to jump in headfirst. However, sometimes the best approach is to ease in slowly and build a new relationship before "breaking up" with the old.

Every transition point in my career was thought out and executed with all parties in mind. After my internship with the Magic, I worked part-time, and then full-time, at WESH. At this point, I also began my freelance career with the Magic Television Network, Sunshine Network, ESPN, TNT, and LMG. When I moved to Tampa a year later, I had built up my freelance network enough to work at WTVT as a part-time employee and gig in Orlando full-time. Yes, that's right. I had a part-time job in Tampa and freelanced full-time in Orlando. I eventually left the news station because more and more opportunities were being offered in Orlando and I was losing money by remaining at my part-time job. So, I made another transition.

The same thing happened after fifteen years of shooting professional sports. Not only was there more opportunity to grow and develop on the corporate/convention side of the industry, but there was more consistent work being offered to me as well. Again, I was losing money by staying. However, this was one of the most difficult decisions I made in my career. I started with the Orlando Magic. With that team, the crew that Rick Price introduced me to back in 2001, I was at home. That's the reason I commuted 192 miles per game and added three hours to my workday. To me, those Cameramen, Directors and Producers, Engineers, Audio and Tape Departments, Camera Utilities, and even the Truck Drivers, were family. They watched me grow from recent college graduate to a newly-married young man. They were there when we began having children, watched me progress from a mentee to a mentor, and looked on while I trained the person who would later take my spot on the court.

This change did not happen overnight. It was gradual and well thought out. This was contemplated with my wife, family, and friends. In the end, I did what was best for all parties involved—I didn't burn any bridges.

FADE IN:
INT: HARROD HOME. TAMPA, FL. DAY

It's 2007 and CLEM is home in Tampa, enjoying a typical day off. He worked the past seven days in Orlando and stayed with a friend who lived in the city. CLEM is lying in his hammock, relieved to finally take a break from his busy lifestyle. CLEM has his phone in his pocket, always ready to receive a call from a scheduling department that might offer him work.

The phone rings. CLEM's heart races anticipating what he's going to be offered next.

                CLEM:
Hello?

                ERIKA:
Hey Clem! It's Erika. I hope you're enjoying your day off.

                CLEM:
I am. Thank you.

CLEM is excited to hear from ERIKA. She always has great opportunities for him.

> ERIKA:
> Good! I heard you did a great job on your last show and that the client was very happy.

> CLEM:
> Oh, yeah? That's awesome!

> ERIKA:
> We'd like to offer you another show tomorrow, if you're available. We had a last-minute cancelation and think you'd be perfect for the job.

> CLEM:
> Sure! I'm always happy to help.

CLEM is already counting and spending the unexpected income.

> ERIKA:
> Perfect! You'll be the Video Projectionist in a large breakout room.

> CLEM:
> Video Projectionist?

There's a long awkward pause. CLEM has never taken the lead role in this position, but he has assisted other Projectionists as a Stagehand. CLEM begins to analyze the situation and understands the catch-22. He could say *no* and someone else could take this spot and opportunity, or CLEM could accept the gig and figure it out.

> CLEM:
> Ok! I'll take it. (CLEM says, knowing he's unsure of what the position fully entails but determined to excel at the task)

> ERIKA:
> Great! We thought you'd be a good fit. I'll send you the details.

CLEM feels a little anxious, but he doesn't want to throw away his shot. CLEM is also wondering who the "We" was ERIKA mentioned in their conversation.

1. CLEM is home in Tampa enjoying a typical day off.

2. CLEM's heart races anticipating what he's going to be offered next.

3. We'd like to offer you another show tomorrow if you're available.

4. Video Projectionist? There's a long awkward pause.

5. OK! I'll take it.

6. CLEM is also wondering who the "We" was ERIKA mentioned in their conversation.

Chapter 3: How Do I Find a Specialty?

My experience in Video and Event Production spanned a large portion of my life by the time I entered the workforce. I was eager, willing to learn and wanted every available opportunity out there. I worked each job position I could—Camera Utility, Score Bug Op., Stagehand, Breakout Technician, Camera Operator, or whatever else that was offered. Then I got a call from the scheduling department asking me to fill in as a Video Projectionist for an event. I was nervous, unsure about what my job would entail, but determined to figure it out. I wasn't afraid to ask questions or to learn from those around me, because I was confident in my ability to navigate the conversation and not become overbearing with my inquisitiveness. It was a gift.

Understand Your Gifts and Talents

There's a reason I picked Communications and Television Production at an early age. Those interests were inherently a part of who I was. From my grandfather, Clement, who enjoyed taking videos and pictures, to my mother, Denise, who left her stable job to follow her passion in photography and recreation, the arts were a part of my DNA. It wasn't chance those things sparked my interest; it was destiny.

God puts gifts inside each and every one of us. It's our job to look within and identify our talents. Once we do, we can master them and learn how they can be of value to others. From there, we can then monetize our time and efforts to produce a product or service that will help society. There's a saying: "If you do what you love, you'll never work a day in your life." I am here to tell you that is absolutely true! I have followed my heart in my career and I have continued to find and make opportunities that fit what I genuinely have to offer and want to give.

> **C.L.E.M. Note**
>
> **The First Steps to Identify Your Gifts:**
>
> - Find a relaxing place
> - Sit and be still
> - Breathe
> - Think about what brings you joy
> - Think about what you do that brings joy to others
> - Write down how the two go hand and hand

The same can be said about my wife. I understand her journey and why she wanted to become a Certified Public Accountant. She just gets it! Numbers make sense to her and she has the discipline to manage them well. She diligently pursued what she loved and now owns a very successful business. She also manages our personal finances as if we were a business ourselves. This was extremely helpful when I was first building my business and had inconsistent cash flow.

Now, I use my understanding of identifying other's gifts and talents as a means to help my son, daughter, and even clients understand how they too can be successful and happy in their lives. Some are mechanically inclined, while others are better at visualizing and creating. Some are better at systems and processes while others enjoy having conversations and connecting with people. The trick is to sit, be still, and assess yourself. Analyze everything about you and how you think. Identify the areas where you are more skilled and where your interests lie. Think about what you would willingly stay up all night working on and what you would be eager to do when you first woke up. It's crazy to think that Video Projection became that for me.

Trusting Others

Sometimes, when you're first starting out, you may not *see* who you are or understand the characteristics you possess that are best for your skill set. In that case, seeking guidance from those you work with is a great first step. Your coworkers, supervisors, and mentors often recognize your strengths and will give you opportunities to build on those skills. Erika Dingman and Steve Campbell did that for me.

When Erika offered me my first Video Projection job, I was unaware of the conversations happening in the background. I didn't realize people were discussing my performance and gradually putting me on jobs that would hone my skills. They were helping me "pro-fect" my craft, and I am so appreciative for what they did. With every opportunity, I was amazed by the scale and magnitude of what we were able to accomplish. I was taken aback by the intricacies of what it took to produce an event. I had a hunger for knowledge and wanted to be around the people who possessed it. I began to realize these jobs were Production, Construction, and Engineering all in one. I began to realize these jobs were me!

I didn't even remember that architecture was an interest from my childhood until I started working with Technical Director, Will Jones, on an event we built in Vegas. I received my drawings/blueprint and equipment list/materials and, step by step, began to write out what I was going to do. Then, step by step again, I began to draw out how I was going to do it. To me, it just made sense to do this pre-planning. I wanted to write these things out in case something went wrong because then I'd know how to fix it. In addition, if something happened to me and I had to leave the job site, then someone could pick up where I left off. Will and I discussed his vision for the event space and I asked him specific questions to deliver what he wanted. I was intrigued. I wanted to see what he saw and envision his desired end result.

That was an amazing moment. Will showed me that I was thinking outside of the box to perfect what was inside it. He helped me identify something within myself I didn't know was there. Will helped me understand that staying up for hours creating my standard operating procedure and thinking of all possible scenarios was not something all Video Projectionists would do. I was different. But to me, I wasn't. I was just Clem. Maybe it was growing up with a mother who was a still photographer and the memory of a grandfather who enjoyed making home movies and doing little woodshop projects. All of that exposure to creativity and production was a part of me. I chose to tap into it and then grow in that space. Because of that choice to be different and true to myself, I love what I do.

Life is too short to be unhappy. If your heart's not in your work, make a choice to change. Make a choice to evolve and make a choice to grow. You won't be successful until you do.

Don't Be Afraid to Get Exposure

Curiosity will expose you to the other aspects and avenues of the industry. Even if you're currently a Stagehand, intentionally look into other departments. Volunteer to help out in every area of the Production. You might go in thinking you're going to like Audio more than Video but then find that your interests truly lie in Scenic Design or Stage Management. You won't know until you take a chance and get that hands-on experience.

I never knew how much I appreciated the Graphics and Content Creation Department until I got to know a very talented individual by the name of Scott Flanigan. Scott wasn't someone I thought I'd hang out with because we seemed so different. He was quiet, more reserved, and a graduate of the University of Florida. Those traits were far from where I was and far from The Florida State University. However, as my desire to increase my knowledge and understanding of Video Projection grew, so did my relationship with Scott. I got to know him beyond the surface, and I began to understand how we would help each other succeed. I encourage you to find new opportunities within your circle of contacts and expand your relationships outside that circle as well.

You never know from where those opportunities will come. Those who have already succeeded and found their area of specialty are tasked with reaching out to help those new to the industry. This is often because their workload has increased due to their professionalism and reputation for delivering great work. These people are often transitioning to new roles, so it is their responsibility to identify new talent to fill their shoes. A prime example of this is Steve Campbell. Steve saw something in me and began pulling strings, knowing he was in a period of transition within the company. I had no idea he was doing this, but now that I am in the same place in my career, I can see what was done. When someone is willing to offer you a new position, they trust you. Give the opportunity a shot. They already believe you can do it—and you should believe you can, too.

> **The Perfect Shot**
>
> I'm a firm believer in face-to-face or over-the-phone interactions rather than impersonal text messages and emails. Some of my best opportunities have come from conversations I've had with people.
>
> I spoke with one potential client about an upcoming fall event and he confirmed me for the gig. The show unfortunately canceled, but we continued to talk even after he had to release me from the event. We got to know each other, and it led to him finding other opportunities for us to work together.
>
> Our interpersonal communication showed him who I was and how invested I became in my projects. Those conversations allowed him to trust me and was a better commercial for my services than any email or social media post

However, if you don't know anyone in the industry or have recently moved to a new area, start networking. I wouldn't be

How Do I Find a Specialty?

where I am today if I didn't get to know people and build relationships. As people got to know and trust me, and saw that I was confident and capable of doing the work, opportunities and connections grew.

Social media is one place where a lot of networking happens, but it's far too easy to rely on a phone or computer and underestimate the value of the human touch. Face-to-face interaction is vital in this industry. People are trusting you with their business and brand. They need to know what kind of person you are and how you will represent them in their absence.

How do you do that? How do you build a rapport and trust? It's as simple as offering to grab a coffee with someone. Get to know them. Learn how to communicate in person. Learn what makes them tick. You'd be surprised how open someone becomes once they realize how much you have in common. I learned this from two phenomenal speakers, Andrá Ward and Reggie Butler. When I was with them, I would just shut up and listen. They were so wise and constantly shared their stories in an effort to help others prosper.

When engaging with people, it's important to know the right time to shut up and listen and the right time to speak. You learn when you're listening. So when you're speaking, you should always ask questions to learn more.

Don't Chase the Money

I know it's tough when you're just starting out, but trust me when I say, "Do NOT focus on the money!" Everyone has bills to pay, I get it. It's often difficult to see potential earnings when you are focused on the bills in front of you. I get that, too. However, there's no amount of money that will make your job gratifying if you don't love the work. Eventually, you'll crack, get fed up, and want to make a change. I know this because I am the product of a parent who cracked. At a certain point, you won't be able to take it anymore, and you'll want your "freedom."

As I've coached professionals transitioning in their careers, I've noticed as they have gradually begun to identify their specialties and embrace their gifts. They didn't recognize either at first because they were chasing the money, but once they reached a level where the money didn't matter, they began chasing their happiness. With the shift in their priorities—happiness over money—the blessing of finances started flowing in. It's funny how that works. As I was building the foundations of my business, I had financial "success," because I was more interested in finding joy and happiness in my work rather than joy and happiness in the things I could consume. That love I had for the industry at the beginning of my career still exists today and is what fuels my passion for teaching and coaching the next generation.

Now, that being said, if you're not making enough money as you transition into your specialty, consider keeping it a hobby—for now. Sometimes, you have to maintain your full-time job, or role, and benefits as you break into something new. When you have a family and a mortgage, you have to be more cautious than someone without those responsibilities. I transitioned from sports to events a little at a time, going from a 90/10 split to 80/20 and so on, until I built up enough work on the event side to leave sports all together. The same thing happened as I transitioned from being a Camera Operator to a Video Projectionist. The key component of that type of switch is forward progress. Diligently work toward your goals. Every day! The forward progress you make will gradually allow you to reduce the work you are doing on one side so you can concentrate on the other.

Level the Scales

If you are branching out into new areas as you find your niche, know that you're going to have an unbalanced life for a while. You will have to juggle the additional workload and your responsibilities at home. My advice to you: *Make time for what's important*. Your happiness will continue to grow as you give your time and energy to something that fulfills you. However, it has to be the right thing that aligns with your long-term success. Once you've found it, life will begin to make more sense. That's when you'll know you've found the area that's perfect for you!

FLASHBACK

It's September 2012, and I'm working a Chipotle managers' meeting at the MGM Grand in Las Vegas, Nevada. Phil Licari is the Head Video Projectionist, and I'm his Assist. In this role, it's my responsibility to be ready and available for whatever Phil needs, and I'm doing just that.

We are setting up a 100'x20' curved screen in the Grand Ballroom and have spent our first day organizing projectors, labeling cables, running them to their destinations, and checking signals. There are over fifty people in the ballroom from various departments including Audio, Video, Lighting, Rigger, Scenic, and even a team building bleachers where the attendees will sit. It's a pretty big show. The second day of load-in is more of the same, but the truss is now at trim, or its designed height, and we are working on projector alignment and programming.

Our ten-hour day is complete, and the majority of the crew has left for the evening. However, now it's our time as the Projection Team to begin the detailed portion of our work—warping. When dealing with a curved screen, though it allows the audience to feel surrounded and engulfed in the experience, there's a trick to executing it properly. You have to manipulate the light source coming out of the projector to make your lines appear straight on a concave or convex surface. This is done through computer programs and an extreme amount of patience and meticulous pinpoint adjustments.

We are approaching the thirteenth hour of our sixteen-hour day, and Phil's computer begins acting up. For whatever reason, his PC is intermittently communicating with, and transferring adjustments to, the six projectors we're using. For three hours, I watch him work on this screen and begin to comprehend how and why he's making those particular adjustments. When Phil's computer finally dies, I offer up my Mac as an alternative. Because of the learning curve between the two operating systems, no pun intended, Phil gives me an opportunity to take over the task of warping and light manipulation.

In that moment, I begin to *see* and embrace a gift. Similar to how I think when I am shooting sports, I notice and understand what moves I should make before I make them. I see the curve, the necessary adjustments, and sense the results for a favorable outcome. This gift isn't something I've been looking for or even something I knew I had, but circumstances allow me to discover it.

Phil continues to coach and encourage me as we work through the night and we are able to complete the alignment within the allotted time. The best part? The client isn't aware of any of the issues we faced, and they are extremely happy with the end result.

Five years later, everything comes full circle when Phil is called in to help me with one of my shows. On the sixteenth hour of my load-in, my Mac stops communicating with the projectors, and Phil and his PC come to my rescue.

These were only two of the many instances where Phil and I worked together throughout my career, but they were instrumental in my development as a Video Projectionist. Phil was my mentor and I will never forget what he taught me.

FADE IN:

INT: MARRIOTT MARQUIS CHICAGO, GRAND HORIZON BALLROOM, CHICAGO, IL. MORNING

It's 2019 and CLEM is working an event for a major automobile manufacturer. His call time is 6am, and CLEM is scheduled to come in early and touch up his 15'x50' widescreen projection image. As part of his daily routine, CLEM listens to inspirational music to get in the proper headspace before he interacts with other crew members and clients. This morning's album was FKJ by French Kiwi Juice. Adjusting the colors and hues in the image, CLEM completes his task just as track seven begins: *Blessed*. CLEM takes a seat in the empty ballroom, stares at his screen's sixteen-step grayscale, and the manufacturer's logo is shining on the kabuki covering the not-yet-released vehicles—a reflection of the amazing opportunity he has been given.

CLEM understands this is a great client and how fortunate he is to work with them. Relationships like these aren't instantly made but fostered over time. CLEM leaves the ballroom and heads to breakfast where he runs into JAY, a former full-time employee who is now a freelancer Audio Engineer.

> CLEM:
> Hey man! How's it going?

> JAY:
> You know, staying busy…

> CLEM:
> Yep. I know.

This is typical AV small talk that doesn't last long in CLEM's conversations.

> CLEM:
> How are you managing the freelance lifestyle?

> JAY:
> Not bad! (Jay says, reflecting on his current situation) Just dealing with these clients and shows. I've got a lot on the books and I'm just prepping for them all. Sometimes I feel like if I can maintain five good clients then I can stay busy.

                    CLEM:
          Yeah, I get that. I feel like I'm
          doing really well if I have three
          busy clients. Trying to maintain
          five clients can be challenging. I
          feel like I'll always be presented
          with shows I can't do.

                    JAY:
          True!

JAY and CLEM both head back to their individual ballrooms and begin working again. Though it wasn't a long conversation, CLEM feels like he left JAY with something to think about.

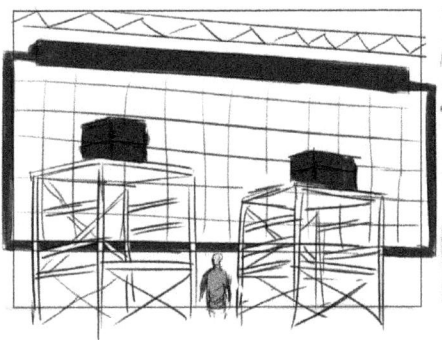

1. His call time is 6am, and CLEM is to come in early and touch up his 15'x50' widescreen projection image.

2. Adjusting the colors and hues in the image, CLEM completes his task just as track seven begins: Blessed.

3. CLEM reflects on the amazing opportunity he has been presented with.

4. I feel like if I can maintain 5 good clients then I can stay busy.

5. I feel like if you get 3 busy clients, then you're doing really well.

6. CLEM felt like he left JAY with something to think about.

Chapter 4
How Do I Build New & Maintain Old Relationships?

Once you start making connections and landing clients, it's important to learn how to maintain the relationships you are building. Sometimes you're juggling two or three clients at a time, and each one of them is important in his or her own way. They each provide different types of opportunities, have different personalities, and require a certain amount of attention. However, it's important to not spread yourself too thin and drop the ball. The last thing you want to do is not be available for one of your clients when they really need you because you are working an event for a different client. It's like being seen at a school dance conversing with a girl at the punch bowl while another is waiting for you on the dance floor. It's a bit awkward and could lead to someone else taking your spot.

I had a lot of these awkward moments the first few years of building my "business." I use the word "business" loosely because it was just me. I was an Independent Contractor and didn't see myself as a business. I saw myself as a guy just trying to make it. I didn't have any subcontractors or employees. All I wanted was to be hired, liked and rehired. I had no idea where to spend my time or focus my energy. I wasn't sure if I should go where I could learn and grow or if I should stay with the sure thing and continue to make enough money to pay my bills. It was just another unknown part of managing the freelance lifestyle. I needed clarity.

Weigh the Opportunity

There will be times when you are asked to work an event for a new client that conflicts with an event you already have booked with an existing one. Before you jump ship to the new opportunity, you need to weigh your options. What are the pros and cons?

> *The current client*: I've worked with these people. They know and trust me, and I know and trust them. I know the ins and outs of their gear. I get a certain number of days with them per year and they're helping me pay my bills and put food on my plate.
>
> *The new client*: It sounds like a cool job, they seem like good people, I could learn a lot, and it could lead to many new opportunities—*but what is their work ethic?* How professional are the events they produce? Will working with them enhance or harm my brand? Are they organized? Will I get the documents and equipment I need for this event or will I spend a lot of time pulling things together? Are they looking for a long-term relationship, or are they interested in a short-term fix?

And, last but not least, will I get paid on time and according to the terms of my invoice?

All of these are unknowns with new clients. You can get references from people who've worked with them, but there are no guarantees. There's an old saying, "It's ten times harder to land a new customer than it is to keep a current one." If you have a great client you already work with, it's important to maintain that relationship. With excellent customer service and gracious follow-ups, you two can grow together. Think of your existing clients as people who are invested in you just as you are invested in them.

How to Say Yes to New Clients

Just the other day, I was requested for a four-day event in Miami, FL. I was grateful for the referral and opportunity. However, before I could say yes and commit to the job, there were a few details I needed to know. I needed to weigh my options:

- I have a great deal of respect for the person who referred me, and I can trust him. Therefore, that trust passes along to the new client and was confirmed after our conversation.
- I haven't seen their equipment, but the projector brands they mentioned and the rental house providing the gear were reputable.
- I let the client know my level of professionalism and the passion I have for each project. They understood and were happy to hear I would care for their event.

- I also let the client know the details and documents I would need to prepare and execute my pre-production, including:

    - Show Name/Number
    - Venue
    - City, State
    - TD/PM Contact Information
    - Equipment List
    - Drawings (.vwx files)

- In the end, I let the client know I would be sending an estimate with my labor policy so there would be no confusion with my rate/terms, and then we could move forward with a mutual understanding.

I know it's uncommon to approach a job with that amount of communication and a labor estimate in my industry. However, I want all assumptions and expectations to be thrown out the window and be replaced with agreements and understandings. I want to do my best to ensure a favorable outcome, provide a quality product, and have the necessary tools to execute my client's vision.

This amount of work and detail comes at a cost and I respect that not everyone is willing to pay it. If a new client is reluctant to pay my full rate, I will consider a small discount. I've done this to build goodwill and establish the relationship, but I let it be known that this is a one-time reduction. I refuse to discount myself too much because my skills and knowledge are valuable. I need to believe this in order to communicate it to the client, and you should too.

My rates have changed over the years because I have built experience, a larger portfolio, and I feel I should charge accordingly for my time. If your skill level hasn't improved much but you are raising your rates, you may want to reconsider. You have to show your value, your worth, and your ability to execute. Taking classes without experience isn't enough to charge more. You have to prove yourself. You have to put in work. I have spent years refining my craft and learning from the best. That is what has gotten me to this point. Not arrogance and entitlement, but humility and appreciation. When I say yes to a project, it's out of a place of gratitude. In my mind, I always think *Thank you for thinking of me and trusting me with your project. Now, I have to deliver*.

How to Say Yes to Old Clients

There isn't much of a challenge here. With old clients, you are established, and they know what they're getting. However, what happens when you've changed your focus and grown in your experience? What happens when you have a new respect for your talents, abilities, and time? What happens when the value of your time has increased?

I have raised my rates for new clients but honored my old rates with existing ones. I have also increased my rate minimally for existing clients to reflect the increased value they receive by hiring me. My clients appreciate this and continue to book me because they can afford my services. I remind myself they too are businesses with overhead and need to make their margins and profits. Yes, I am a part of their revenue stream, and that's okay. I get it. But they also have to understand that my time and expertise are of value.

I also charge for travel days. Those days I'm on a plane or driving across the state, are days I'm not working or spending time with my family. As I stated, it's all about knowing your value and worth. Because my jobs are typically out of town and not in my home city, my rate is based on a twenty-four-hour day. What is my time worth to be away from, and unavailable to, my family for twenty-four hours? I know clients are basing things off an eight or ten-hour workday and then overtime is calculated accordingly, but my business model is different. I am a husband and father first, and that's where my priorities lie. As a business owner, I am constantly faced with booking request conflicts. I have lost several jobs and opportunities, one of them being in Dublin, Ireland, because they didn't fit our family's schedule. It was very difficult to say, "I'm not available," but my family came first. I know everyone's situation is different. We don't all have the same responsibilities or priorities. The most important thing is to maintain balance.

Another way I say yes to clients is through offering my pre-production services. I thoroughly enjoy spending time pre-planning an event, thinking about the best execution strategies, and documenting each step. It's like building the show in my mind, then going onsite and recreating what I've already seen. Some would call this an exercise in manifestation, or the act of making something real and tangible.

Pre-production isn't something most clients would typically pay for because it may not be included in their initial budget.

However, after I demonstrated the value in reviewing the drawings, equipment list, production schedule, etc., my clients began to notice the amount of time I saved on site. I became more efficient. I was able to catch mistakes prior to beginning the build, thus saving time and money.

My pre-production time has had a direct impact on the success of events. It's a proven method. However, not all clients want to see that extra charge on their invoices. In such cases, I build that expense into my hourly rate. I know I'm charging what I'm worth and for the value I'm bringing to the table. People who aren't willing to pay my rate either don't see my value or don't understand my brand. I care about every show and that's why I dedicate so much time and effort to them.

> **C.L.E.M. Note**
>
> **Diversify your portfolio.**
>
> It's important to rely on more than one company or personal skill set to pay your bills. The 2009 economy shift affected the convention market, and various NBA and NHL lockouts have affected my job offerings as well. These were financially challenging times that I had to maneuver and navigate through. By having a variety of service items and clients, it made life easier.
>
> Things happen and having multiple revenue streams helps you guard against disaster. Think of them as income redundancies.

How to Say No

There will come a point in your career when you are being offered more jobs than you have time. When you reach that juncture, saying *no* may be very difficult.

I have been very fortunate and blessed. Work has steadily been available, and I have been building a career and living a life beyond my dreams. My clients appreciate my work and I have enjoyed assisting them on every project. However, my time on site has drastically decreased. My family has grown, and thus my priorities have shifted. I am no longer available to work fifteen to twenty days on the road per month. At the same time, my client's businesses have grown, and their demands are greater. Shows are getting bigger, more complicated, and the destinations are becoming more extravagant. They need qualified technicians and are asking me for my help. What do I do?

Some of the most challenging offers I've received came from one of my mentors, Steve Campbell. As a former Video Projectionist, and now Vice President of Live Events for an industry-leading company, when Steve called, I knew I was needed. It was extremely difficult, but there were times I had to say, "I'm sorry. I can't," and it hurt. I wanted to be there for him—not because I felt like I owed him, but because I wanted to thank him for all he'd done for my career.

When you are offered an opportunity that conflicts with a current event on your calendar, work-related or not, how you handle saying *no* can make a world of difference. Saying, "I'm not available," could be a deciding factor whether or not you are hired in the future. You have to know your audience. Or in this case, you have to know your client. We all have different approaches and ways we communicate. Some people like for you to be direct and to the point, while others would prefer to know and understand why there's a conflict.

I was having a conversation with Joe Freeman, a labor coordinator I've known almost my entire career, about this very subject. Joe is happy with an "I'm not available." He and his team realize the technicians they contact are Independent Contractors and have other clients. "I'm not available" allows them to move on and continue the search. Joe did state what he values most are technicians who don't overextend themselves and double book. Your word is your bond. If you've committed to an event, then you should be available and prepared to work it.

For clients who prefer a less-direct approach, it's all about developing soft skills. These would be clients with whom you have a better rapport and friendlier relationship. These clients enjoy a more open line of communication and tend to be more flexible. Telling these clients, "Unfortunately, I have another commitment that day. I wish I was available. Please keep me in mind for the next one," is a more likely reply. Even letting clients know the dates you have as a conflict out of a week's worth of work could be helpful. If the conflicting date is only one out of seven, then there's a possibility the schedule could be adjusted, and things could work out. You don't want to miss an opportunity through a lack of communication.

At the same time, you don't want to overcommunicate. I would not recommend telling a client you aren't available because you are working for their competitor, going to a sporting event, or just want to sit home and take some time off. Yes, as an Independent Contractor, you work for yourself, and you have the right to set your own schedule. However, you want to make sure your client knows you appreciate their offer. We all have lives outside of work, and we can't let the demands of the industry consume our time and cause us to neglect our obligations. We need balance.

If someone requests you for a date and you have plans or obligations where someone else is depending on you, you aren't available. It's as simple as that. I understand the catch-22 that another technician may take your spot and you may lose a week of work or a client. I've heard it all before. In fact, I lived it. I was nervous and uncertain about receiving those calls, but when I began to focus on the jobs I had instead of the jobs I didn't, everything changed. More opportunities came once I concentrated on making my current clients happy instead of thinking about the next one. It's like going back to that school dance with the girl at the punch bowl. Enjoy your time there and give her your full attention. When you are done, make your way to the floor and see if that dance is still available.

But what happens when you don't want to dance, and you want to leave? I've had those situations, too. If you find yourself at an event you no longer want to work or doing a position you no longer want to fill, tough it out for the rest of the contract. Then, use your soft skills to turn down future opportunities that may come your way. This is a very small industry and you could end up working with that client again down the road. Saying something like, "I appreciate the offer. Unfortunately, I'm no longer taking jobs in X position and I've moved on to Y. Please keep me in mind for opportunities in that area," could work in your favor.

The #1 Key to Building Good Relationships

Be of good character. That means be on time and professional. Be the problem solver. Be that can-do, how-can-I-assist person everyone knows and likes. If you do those things, you will find clients that best suit you, and you them. It may take some time, but they're out there. Trust and have faith that you all will meet and grow together.

Be of good character for the client you no longer work with: If you turn down a job because it's not right for you, don't just say *no* and walk away. Be a problem solver. Recommend another technician who can fill their need. The client will appreciate you attempted to solve their problem and they will remember you for that.

Be of good character with your words: You don't want to be remembered as someone who creates a toxic and unproductive work environment. Be mindful of your surroundings and how you speak of people and companies. Your words can affect your reputation and the reputation of others. If you're a person who complains all the time, clients, and possibly other technicians, won't want you around. On the other hand, if you are a person of good character who's

> **The Perfect Shot**
>
> The policy of a company I often work with is to have a full-time employee on-site when they rent out gear. As a Freelancer, I built my reputation and character on being a reliable, trustworthy person.
>
> Therefore, it was no surprise when I was asked to go onsite as a Freelancer and represent the company when they sent out a 15'x50' Stewart Screen to a new customer. They knew I would take care of the equipment and provide a service that represented their brand well.
>
> Now, I help supply labor for that same company in my market. My values, principals, and respect for the event are things I pass along to my techs. If my character was in question, that opportunity would have never come to fruition.

efficient and has a great work ethic, word will spread, and work will come your way.

Be of good character for those who will follow in your footsteps: I'm where I am today because someone put my name forward. I try to do the same for the subcontractors who work for me and whom I coach and mentor. In fact, my company often helps them put together a resume and portfolio as a service, because those things are just as important. When I recommend someone, the client knows that person represents my brand. Thus, I make sure every recommendation is a good one.

It's Always About Your Brand

As you grow your business, whether you are a Sole Proprietor or an LLC with employees and subcontractors, everything you choose to do should be indicative of the kind of company and business you are building. If your brand is professional, clean cut, and understated, then choosing the corporate and live events that match that image makes sense. If your brand is rough around the edges, aggressive, and get-in-there-and-get-it-done-no-matter-what, then a roadie lifestyle and image may suit you better. Once you know your brand, you can tap in and increase your network across that space.

The most important thing I've learned about building and maintaining relationships in my professional life is to retain the balance and peace in my personal life. Work, family, friends, personal reflection, and my relationship with God, are all aspects of who I am. I like to think of it as a bar graph where if

How Do I Build New & Maintain Old Relationships?

everything were balanced, they would all equal 20%. It seems ideal, but that's never the case. Something will always take priority at one time or another.

For the past two weeks, I've been on the road working the event for the automotive company I previously mentioned. While I've been gone, my time with my family and friends has suffered. I've been able to make time for my personal and spiritual reflection, but I'm longing for that balance. It's a part of my brand. It's a part of my principals and my character. These things help me decide which jobs to take and what relationships to maintain. If you understand the scales and bar graph early in your career, you too will be able to prioritize your relationships.

FLASHBACK

In the summer of 2002, when I completed my internship, I started my job at WESH-TV. During that time, I freelanced with the Magic, The Miracle (the local WNBA team) and LMG working conventions. I describe that season of my life as burning the candle on both ends *with* a wick sticking out and burning in the middle. My schedule at WESH was from 4am to 1pm, then I would leave there and go work a Magic game from 1:30pm to 10pm multiple days a week. When there wasn't a game, I tried to find convention work as well. I was working hard in three different areas, trying to stay diverse and build relationships.

I never desired a career in the news industry, but it was a full-time job that could pay my bills and put food on the table. It was guaranteed income. During the NBA lockout, I started doing more convention work because no games were being broadcasted. Around the time of the housing market crash, corporations scaled back on lavish events, so I went back to more sporting events. Multiple eggs in multiple baskets meant I always had an income stream and a way to keep building my business.

This could not have been done without maintaining the relationships I had built. The Crewers at the various companies knew me and knew I was dedicated to their events. They knew I managed a schedule with jobs in markets all across the state. *But I never made them feel neglected.* I always did my best to make them feel like they were my priority, because when I was on their job, I was focused on their job. Take care of people and they will take care of you.

Act II:
The Show

You are in the groove and progressing, but there's more to learn and understand. You can live this life better.

FADE IN:

INT: SPARE BEDOOM IN HARROD HOME, TAMPA, FL. AFTERNOON

The kids are in school, and CLEM is arguing with his wife about finances. She found the bag of clothes CLEM was hiding in the guest bathroom shower. CLEM has been buying items and hiding them to avoid arguments about his spending habits. As his wife makes point after point about the bags of clothes, CLEM begins to think maybe he does have a problem with budgeting, saving, and using money as a valuable resource.

CLEM calls BRIAN, whom he'd met during a *Make it Snappy Productivity Show* podcast interview. CLEM asks BRIAN for a referral of someone who can help him manage his finances. BRIAN gives CLEM the phone number of professional bookkeeper, BOBBI GRANT.

> BOBBI:
> Hello, this is Bobbi. (BOBBI says with a sweet southern-like charm and uplifting sound emphasizing the "i" in her name)

CLEM:
Hello?

CLEM is taken aback by the pleasant tone that greets him on the phone during his time of frustration.

BOBBI:
Hi! How can I help you? (BOBBI says with that same uplifting, welcoming and confident voice)

CLEM:
Brian said I should give you a call. I need some help with my finances. (CLEM says, nervous and embarrassed)

BOBBI:
Yes, I've been expecting your call. Tell me about your situation.

CLEM:
Well, I'm an Independent Contractor and I'm having a difficult time managing my finances with inconsistent cash flow. Can you help me?

> BOBBI:
> I certainly can. I taught classes on this subject and I'd be happy to help you.

> CLEM:
> For years, my wife tried to teach me these same principles, but something prevented me from learning them from her. Thank you for helping me, Bobbi. I greatly appreciate this.

Tears come to CLEM's eyes as he feels he is finally getting the help he needs.

> BOBBI:
> You are quite welcome, Clem.

CLEM, still holding the phone, begins feeling grateful and relieved that he can start getting things on the right track.

1. She found the bag of clothes CLEM was hiding in the guest bathroom shower.

2. CLEM asks BRIAN for a referral of someone who can help him manage his finances.

3. Hello, this is Bobbi.

4. CLEM says nervously and embarrassed.

5. Well, I'm an independent contractor, and I am having a difficult time managing my finances with inconsistent cash flow.

6. CLEM begins feeling grateful and relieved that he can start getting things on the right track.

Chapter 5

How Do I Set Up a Budget?

I'd been freelancing for many years and earning a comfortable wage. I had a new car with twenty-inch chrome rims and the ability to purchase anything I wanted from the outlet malls I frequented in Orlando. After growing up impoverished in Miami, I had dreamed of having this kind of spending ability, but it took me a while to realize I was unsuccessfully chasing happiness. I was constantly working to pay off the debt I incurred the previous month, and it was and taking a toll on my marriage.

My wife, a Certified Public Accountant, understands numbers and finances unlike anyone I know. I jokingly say she's able to take ten cents and turn it into a dollar. Financial security is her world, and I was ruining it. I was taking away, and challenging, the very sense of stability she fought her whole life to achieve because of my need for instant gratification. I needed to change how I viewed and used money to achieve my goals, but part of my problem was that I didn't *have* any goals.

Setting Goals for What You Want

Bobbi said something in our first meeting that really stuck with me: "You have to imagine a life you want. Beyond the material things and beyond what you see others obtaining, lies your happiness. There lie your dreams and goals. All of that starts with hard work, determination, and a budget." I was on track with the first two items on the list, but I didn't have a budget to help me create my ideal image. It's like producing an event and knowing how you want it to look and what equipment you need but having no idea what it's going to cost or how you are going to afford it.

One of the most important things you will need as an Independent Contractor or small business owner is a budget. Without one, you can quickly get into financial trouble. By creating a budget, you are telling your money where it will be spent, and not the other way around. By creating a budget, you are thinking about how much you have coming in and what you can afford to send out. Whether you are thinking

> **C.L.E.M. Note**
>
> **Follow a purchase plan.**
>
> If you want something for yourself or your business, you should take the following steps before spending money:
>
> - research options
> - price them out
> - make a decision
> - work to earn income
> - set aside money from your checks
> - track your savings
> - reach your goal
> - purchase desired item
> - set a new goal

about your business or your family, creating and maintaining a budget is your responsibility.

Understand Your Wants Versus Your Needs

There's a difference between wants and needs, and often that line is blurred. We live in a time where we are inundated with information and flashy objects. We are constantly shown lifestyles that look "great." My question is, are they *truly* great or are they what corporations want us to see and think? Are these trips, cars, homes, and fancy phones needed? Are they paid for, or are people indebted to them? I grew up poor, and I wasn't responsible with money when I first started making it.

I didn't know *how* to be fiscally responsible. I was never taught how to plan for the future. I was never taught how to research something I wanted, price it out, work at my job, set aside money from my checks, save up, and purchase the desired item. Because we didn't have money, everything was placed on a credit card, then the minimum balance was paid until there was enough room on the card to buy the next thing. This was a vicious cycle that wasn't leading to success.

I needed to learn to be patient and wait, and I needed to stop looking for instant gratification. During the time I was spending frivolously, I felt like I had an endless stream of jobs. I didn't think there would be a day when things would shift, or I might want to cut back and someday stop working. I was extremely happy with my career and every day was better than the next. However, I was working more hours than I needed to because I wouldn't stop spending the money I earned. In addition to buying what I wanted, I still had the responsibility to contribute to the household bills, and I was under constant pressure. I was spending more and more time away from my wife and kids because I was buying the things I *wanted* and not the things I *needed*. I didn't prioritize my money; therefore, I wasn't prioritizing my time. My actions literally said the things I wanted to buy were more important than spending time at home with my family.

Again, I understand that isn't everyone's situation; not everyone has a spouse and kids to worry about. Either way, the principle remains the same. **The amount of money you spend on something reflects the amount of time you give up in order to purchase it**. Your rate and wage are a reflection of how much your time is worth. Therefore, when an item has a large dollar amount associated with it, you may want to calculate how much of your time it will take to pay for it, alongside your other expenses.

I began to embrace this level of understanding once I introduced a neutral third party into my finances. These are things my wife tried to tell me, but when she said words like *accruing funds,* I just didn't get it. She was simply saying I needed to set aside money from every check to pay for my monthly, quarterly, and yearly bills. This also included setting aside money for leaner times of the year. Bobbi and my wife both recommended saving enough cash for at least six months' worth of bills. "When an economic downturn comes, you, and everyone else, will be scrambling to find work," they would say. So, I took their advice and began to prepare. I set my first goal.

How to Set Up a Budget

I can't stress enough how vital a budget is for your home and business. It is the scaffolding for every single decision you will make. Without a budget, you won't know if you can afford new equipment, an office space, or whether or not you can take some time off work. Once I began to understand the value of my time, and how much of it I was giving up by my lack of discipline and poorly managed priorities, I realigned my focus.

This might seem like basic information, but you would be surprised how many people, including myself at one point, don't understand this concept or know how to do it. As an Independent Contractor, you don't have a paycheck coming in every two weeks. Your next job isn't guaranteed, and it can be nearly impossible to forecast work months in advance. Therefore, a budget is essential for stability and sustainability.

Bobbi recommends these steps:
1. Print out the last three to six months' worth of bank and credit card statements.
2. Make a list of categories, or buckets, for your expenses (I prefer Excel, but some banks do this on your statements): Electricity, Rent, Equipment, Travel, Meals, etc.
3. Make sure every dollar you've spent goes into a specific bucket. You shouldn't have anything left over or labeled miscellaneous.
4. Total each category.
5. Divide those numbers by the number of months you are analyzing (preferably six months).

6. This creates your basic budget. You can now use the CLEMCO.U Basic Budget Template, available at www.clemcohr.com, or another application to plan for that amount of expenditures in each category.
7. Analyze these expenses against your monthly income. Are you spending more than you make?
8. Evaluate the amount of money you are choosing to spend in each category and decide if you should make adjustments to your spending.

It's really that simple. You are looking at the numbers and collecting data. Then, you use that information to make analyses, forecasts, and estimates of how much you will need each month to stay in the positive. You are also seeing what emotionally drives you to spend your money. For me, it was the desire to be accepted and happy. Purchasing clothes and things filled that void but, after looking at my budget, I realized I was setting myself up for failure.

Now, create your own budget. Look at your numbers. Analyze them. What you

> **The Perfect Shot**
>
> "I believe the children are our future. Teach them well, and let them lead the way . . ." Those lyrics in Whitney Houston's song *Greatest Love of All* are very true in life. My ten-year-old son recently worked an event with me. I paid him $50 for his time and effort. I know I overpaid, but he's my son. LOL
>
> After he received his cash, we discussed percentages. How much are you giving to the church, or your charitable contribution? How much is going into savings for your future self, and how much are you keeping for the present day?
>
> He's ten, but I wanted him to understand these concepts early and build a strong foundation for when he's making these decisions as an adult.

choose to do with that information is up to you.

It's easy to spend unnecessarily—going out to eat instead of making your meals and buying things you want when there's a surplus. It's also easy to tell yourself "you've earned it" after working hard on an event. That's how I felt and what I did because I never foresaw an end to the income stream. I never felt the need to save. That kind of thinking could have gotten me into a lot more trouble if I hadn't woken up to the need for structure and a budget.

What to Do With the "Extra" Money

If you have more income than expenses, that's great! That's how it should be. That means you understand the value of your money, and you have the discipline to manage your wants versus your needs. Save this additional money. Build your emergency fund. Total up your expenses for six months and know how much you need. Now, save until you have that cushion set aside for the times when work is scarce. You will need it. Trust me.

Before I was a W-2 employee of my company, I was a Sole Proprietor. Whenever I received payment for a job, I set aside 10% of my gross income for a cushion, 25% for taxes, and 5% for a minimal retirement savings. Those expenses came off the top. The remaining amount, my net, was 60% of my check and I had learned to work within that remaining budget. You can see an example of this on the previously mentioned CLEMCO.U Basic Budget Template.

My wife and I began building this template many years ago as we learned to manage my inconsistent cash flow. It has been an invaluable and evolving tool that has encouraged me to be more mindful and intentional with the money I earn. Because of it, and because of what she's taught me, I really try to think before I make any major purchases and always keep an eye on the future.

How to Keep Track

In the beginning, my business was small enough that I could use an Excel spreadsheet to keep track of incoming and outgoing money. As things grew, I made the switch to QuickBooks. Although there are several software options out there, it is important to look for one that fits the way you work. QuickBooks, though intimidating at first, allows me to invoice and collect payments directly from the app. It also syncs with my business banking and credit card accounts, sorts and categorizes my expenses as they come in, and, best of all, allows my accountant to have direct access to all of this information. As I said, other applications allow for this as well, but I really enjoy QuickBooks' workflow. I feel it suits the way I think.

Another benefit to QuickBooks is its ability to capture your receipts and add them to your categorized expenses. Every accountant I've had says you should save your receipts and maintain a log of what the purchases were for. The IRS doesn't like vagueness and being able to prove you spent $12.73 on file folders and pens is a lot better than saying "miscellaneous office items." Fortunately, I haven't had any issues with the IRS, and the plan is to make sure I keep things in order to not have any in the future.

Sticking to the Budget

Many of us use credit cards to pay for purchases because we want to earn travel miles and points to achieve "status." While those perks are great, it can become invisible money. Meaning, you are spending it without thinking about it. Then the bill comes and the money you worked so hard to earn flies right out the window. Speaking from personal experience, it's difficult to keep track of your purchases and exhibit discipline when everything you buy is a quick signature.

The alternative? Pay with cash. Cash is something you visually and intellectually process as you are counting it out for your bills and purchases. There's something about holding that currency in your hand and watching it deplete that will cause you to rethink your decisions and restrict your purchases.

One of the things I do when traveling and working an event is short myself the per diem. Instead of spending the allocated $65 per day to cover living expenses, I only spend $50 or less and treat it like a game to save money. By doing this, I've learned that it's possible to restrict my spending and my family and I benefit from the extra cash. In fact, as I am writing this my wife and I are returning from an anniversary trip to Rome where I used my extra per diem to pay for our meals and excursions. This is something I never imagined or thought I'd be able to do. Keeping track of that cash in an envelope allowed me to manage and grow that money, separate from my bank account, and return from our trip debt-free.

You, too, can separate your budgeted items, or buckets, into different envelopes of cash. You will see how this can not only help you keep track of your spending, but also save money. When I do it, I will literally write my withdrawals and deposits on the envelope. This is sometimes a necessary step in the beginning. It helps you form good habits and ensures you aren't leaving yourself, and your business, short of funds.

Don't get me wrong. Credit cards aren't a bad thing if you are disciplined with your spending. In fact, they are an essential part of doing business. My wife and I were recently discussing the importance of being able to pay for things like venue parking, hotel incidentals, airfare and even meals as you await reimbursement from a client for a job you've worked. Not everyone has the capital available to float those expenses and using a debit card can be an inconvenience with the holds businesses put on the cash in your bank account. A credit card can provide both flexibility and security when used properly. As long as you are responsible, a credit card can help you and your business grow.

Making a Lot of Money?

Financial planning and deciding what type of business you want to be—a Sole Proprietorship, a LLC, or an S/C corporation—are very important. However, to get to that point you need to make money.
I love working in the Live Event Production Industry, and I make a great wage doing it. But I have no formal education in business forecasting and planning. To figure things out, I hired an accountant who specializes in those areas to help me sort

through the various details. As I mentioned, budgets, balance sheets, accruals, and reconciliation were all foreign words my wife used when discussing her business and making reference to mine. I was clueless. However, after I retired from shooting sports and shifted my focus to corporate events, I realized I needed to develop a plan. I needed to set goals for my future. Retiring from one sector of the industry while transitioning into another helped me see who and where I was. It also helped me understand where I wanted to be. To reach my goal, I needed to start working with my accountant and financial planner to develop a roadmap for my success.

A good accountant is worth the expense. Don't skimp on paying for the service of a true professional. I've had three different CPAs and I am married to one. They will help you stay on track financially and also help you keep your books organized should the IRS want to audit your business.

That being said, choose an accountant who fits your business at the time, but realize you may need to make a change in the future. I read a book by Les Goldberg, founder and CEO of LMG, and he stated the people who can help you take your company from $1 million to $10 million may not be the same people who take your company from $10 million to $25 million. I'm paraphrasing his advice a bit, but that stuck with me. The type of accountant you hire when your business is grossing $25,000 a year may be different from the type of accountant you hire when your business is grossing $250,000 a year. I have worked with different accounting firms over the years because my business grew and my financial needs changed. Don't be afraid to move on to someone who offers the level of service and advice that you need.

Charitable Contributions

A large part of my budget is devoted to helping other Independent Contractors and Freelancers get their foot in the door, as well as to help them develop their skills and understand different aspects of businesses. To me, giving back is as important as earning, and I build that into my budget. How all that translates from an accounting and tax standpoint is left to the professional, but I made the decision to make it a priority. I understand that giving to others will help me achieve my desired future and dream—one where I see people who are encouraged and empowered to step out on their own and are given the tools and resources for long-term success.

What Do You Want?

I challenge you. Take a moment, be still, and ask yourself, "What *do* I want for my future?" Whatever it is, a budget is the first step to obtaining it. With the help of the right tools and professionals, you can build a budget that offers security for the days ahead.

The more you are a part of the budgeting process and knowing where your business stands at any given moment, the better off you are. This is *your* business. You need to be a good steward of what you have—appreciate the blessings that have been, and will continue to be, poured into your company.

Visit www.clemcohr.com to discover our Basic Budget Template and some of the service providers available to assist you.

FLASHBACK

It was October 2019. I was working with my new accountant, and I had been using QuickBooks for three years. I had a good grasp of the application and had maintained very organized financials, thanks to my CPA wife. Entering the fourth quarter of the year, my accountant wanted to schedule our annual review and budgeting session. I was nervous and unsure of what to expect, because all I could think about was those first meetings with previous accountants where I was lost and had a fear of creating a budget. However, I knew it was something I had to do.

We talked about the previous and current year's trends, then discussed obtainable *goals* for the following year. "Goals?!" I'd never set goals. Up to that point, I had only thought about the next job and managing opportunities as they arose. I was intrigued and thoroughly enjoyed the process of looking at past numbers, seeing the growth, and creating projections based off the data. It was so freeing to think that I was in control. I was, essentially, the master of my fate. You can be too!

Don't be afraid to sit down with a professional to discuss how to better manage your money. It's a game changer!

FADE IN:
INT: ACCOUNTANT'S OFFICE, ST PETERSBURG, FL. DAY

It is February 2005, and CLEM and his wife realize they should bring in a professional to help file their taxes. It seems odd because CLEM's wife is a Certified Public Accountant, but CLEM understands her thought processes.

Yes, CLEM is a Camera Operator, but he doesn't shoot all types of events. He could, but sometimes it's best to find someone who specializes in that area. In their case, they want someone who understands small business accounting and knows the best strategy when it comes to not only paying taxes but creating an entity.

Though the entity creation wasn't on CLEM's mind, he felt meeting with this particular firm was the right thing to do. They were already servicing individuals and small businesses in his industry and might be the best fit for CLEM and his family.

                JOHN:
Good Afternoon! Come on in. So, I hear you know Bob, Tom, and Trina.

CLEM:
Yes. We work together shooting sports.

JOHN:
Oh yeah! Which ones?

CLEM:
Lightning, Rays, Bucs Pre-Season and whoever else comes to town. (CLEM chuckles) Living that 1099 Lifestyle…

They both have a good laugh, which helps to break the ice a bit.

JOHN:
1099 indeed.

There's a brief pause as JOHN begins to think about the numerous W9 and 1099 Forms CLEM is dealing with on a yearly basis.

JOHN:
So, how can I help?

                    CLEM:
          Well, my wife and I need someone who
          gets my industry and can help us
          file our taxes.

                    JOHN:
          Okay. What is your gross annual
          income?

                    CLEM:
          Excuse me?

CLEM looks very confused. He clearly has no
idea what JOHN's asking.

                    JOHN:
          How much money are you making per
          year?

                    CLEM:
          I have no idea. Probably about
          thirty. (CLEM looks up, trying to
          visualize his earning in his mind)
          Yeah, that's right. About $30,000.

CLEM has never thought about how much he's
actually bringing in each year. He's only
thought month to month. His focus is his
current job, the next one, and putting the

necessary amount into the joint bank account.

> JOHN:
> Okay. That's a start. I'll ask you a few more questions, but eventually we may want to consider setting you up as an LLC.

CLEM has no idea what that is or what it means, but he sees Bob, Tom, and Trina's success as veterans in the industry and figures, "If it works for them, then it may work for me."

1. CLEM felt meeting with this particular firm was the right thing to do.

2. (CLEM chuckles) Living that 1099 Lifestyle…

3. Ok, what is your Gross Annual Income?

4. CLEM looks very confused. He clearly has no idea what JOHN's asking.

5. How much money are you making per year?

6. "if it works for them, then it may work for me."

Chapter 6
How Do I Decide on a Business Model?

I was in business for about fifteen years before I realized I needed to become more structured with my business model. While interning with the Orlando Magic, the only thing I wanted was to become a W2 employee of the organization. That meant I would have a schedule and routine similar to the one I had for that 2001-2002 season, get paid an hourly wage or salary for my work and have my taxes and 401K retirement funds taken out of my check for me. That's all I knew existed, so that's what I wanted. My mind couldn't conceive of anything different. I was unaware of a 1099 lifestyle because everyone I knew lived a W2 one. Now, however, I get it. I understand how, for some companies, it's better to have an intern- or subcontractor-heavy business model. In order to have full-time employees on staff, you must have enough work/clients to support paying them *and* what's owed to the government on their behalf. Therefore, it is cheaper and easier to use contractors than carry all that overhead. I also now understand how important it is for

Independent Contractors to be aware of the details of their own business model so they can best provide for themselves.

In my line of work, being a 1099 contractor made the most sense (meaning I wasn't on my client's payroll; they paid me as a subcontractor and then issued a 1099 at the end of the year). It was just easy. For both parties, it required minimal paperwork, and as long as I kept my business account separate from my personal, it was relatively easy to file my taxes. That option works for many small businesses, but you should consider alternative models for long-term success as you grow.

Income vs. Salary

If you are aware of your budget, income, and expenditures, you should also be aware of your annual income and your own salary. I wasn't when I first started. I never thought to look at the money I was paid as a contractor as income or the money I paid myself as a wage or a salary. As a business entity, there's a big difference in the way you should operate. However, one must see themselves as an entity to comprehend this. For me, the trick was to look at myself in the third person. I am Clem, but I am also CLEMCO.AV. Sounds weird, doesn't it? Yeah, it sounded weird to me, too. But

> **C.L.E.M. Note**
>
> **Step Outside of Yourself**
>
> Being a successful entrepreneur or business owner means seeing yourself in the third person. You are an employee of your idea, skill, or service. Your gift is able to be given or sold as a means to support you and provide a wage or salary.
>
> *See* yourself to provide for yourself.

that's what I needed to *see* to begin better managing my finances.

When there's a job opportunity, a client reaches out to CLEMCO.AV for support. CLEMCO.AV then hires Clem Harrod to do the job. CLEMCO.AV receives income for the work, and Clem Harrod receives a salary for the work he did that month for CLEMCO.AV. Make sense?

At the end of the day, I was the only one providing the service, but I was also responsible for scheduling, invoicing, bill collecting, payroll, and new client acquisition/sales. Wearing every hat was very challenging, but I loved it. I was living my passion. I worked to figure it all out because that's how my industry was set up and I didn't want to be anywhere else. Facing this challenge forced me to exercise the right and left sides of my brain to create something sustainable—a successful business.

As my income and salary increased, I was advised to meet with my accountant and financial planner to determine whether it was time to incorporate and adjust my business model. When your numbers increase, and they will, you should consider meeting with an accountant as well. These are notable accomplishments in your life and business. It's of the utmost importance to get experienced counsel before making any major decisions.

The following are business verbiage and classifications to help you establish basic understanding:

Independent Contractor

An Independent Contractor provides a service for a customer but is not classified as an employee. This service (rather than a product) sold to a customer should be free from the control of the payee. According to the "Independent Contractor Defined" page of the United States Internal Revenue Service, this means "... the payer has the right to control or direct only the result of the work and not what will be done and how it will be done."

This reminds me of work I do for one of my favorite clients, Nick Farrell. Nick is a very creative person and always has an idea. When planning my work as a Video Projectionist and the execution of my build, I always leave room for the "Nick Factor." He is very genuine and diplomatic about his ask, but I know that something will always need a tweak. A screen "could move" a little left or a little right, a little up or a little down. He's not telling me what to do or how to do it, but he is suggesting how he would like the end result to look and feel. Knowing the "Nick Factor" exists, I always leave room in my planning for his input.

I would suggest using a contract when working with a client to ensure that deliverables are met on both ends. This eliminates the expectation aspect of the relationship and turns it into a legal agreement. In that same regard, the agreement your client has with the federal government is to report your income and issue you a Form 1099 if you are paid more than $600 in one calendar year. Regardless of whether they do that, you are expected to report your income to the IRS. For this reason, you should keep very accurate records and consider using the CLEMCO.U Basic

Budget Template, QuickBooks or a similar application. You should also consider opening a dedicated business checking and credit/debit card account so that your business and personal funds are separated.

Patrick Murtha, a partner at Murtha & Murtha, LLC, says contractors need to realize they are responsible for both sides of the tax bill. When you work for a company, typically your employer pays half and you pay the other half of this expense each pay period. As an Independent Contractor, however, "you need to be prepared to pay both federal income tax as well as self-employment (SE) tax." The IRS accepts estimated payments on a quarterly schedule, or annual payments with an added penalty fee. There may be additional tax obligations depending on your state residency, but I recommend working with a creditable accountant to estimate payments and remain in good standing with the government.

Sole Proprietorship

According to Entrepreneur.com, "The sole proprietorship is the simplest business form under which one can operate a business. The sole proprietorship is not a legal entity. It simply refers to a person who owns the business and is personally responsible for its debts." A key takeaway is that you do not have to be a separate legal entity to own and operate a business. A single person can be a business, including an Independent Contractor who provides services. However, a Sole Proprietorship can also be a person who sells a product.

There was a girl in my community who used to take old baseballs and create personalized key chains from them. She had the idea after attending a countless number of her brother's games. With her dad, she figured out the steps and cost to manufacture the product in their garage, and the price point to sell it and make a profit. Something so simple turned into a profitable business without obtaining an Employer Identification Number (EIN) and forming a corporation. There was no "Doing Business As" (DBA) form filed and no business bank account opened, but they still had an opportunity to be a business. They turned a fun craft project from a hobby into a business because they earned money.

That being said, if someone felt the need to pursue the girl and hold her liable for any legal issues, they would be going after her personally because she didn't put the available legal protections into place. In addition, without a separate business account in the name of a legal entity, her assets, and possibly her family's as well, would be in jeopardy. Mind you, I am not an attorney, but these are all things to consider with any venture.

Going into business is an assessment of risk versus opportunity. If your reward outweighs your risk and you can manage the process, you could potentially have a profitable business.

It's always best to seek the guidance of a professional when considering what business model best suits you and your idea.

Limited Liability Company

Becoming an LLC is the next step up from being a Sole Proprietor and creates a solid line between your business and

How Do I Decide on a Business Model?

your personal assets. This type of company, which is filed on the state and federal level, allows the government and courts of law to recognize the entity if an incident were to occur where the business, or someone within, was at fault. As the owner of the company, this type of separation could be in the best interests of you and your family. When you are an LLC, your personal finances typically aren't on the line for your business debts. Some banks do tie the two together, so always ask questions when you apply for a business loan to ensure that your personal assets aren't liable. Scott Hewitt, Esq., an attorney with Mandlebaum, Fitzimmons, Hewitt, & Cain P.A., said having an LLC, "... means you are individually protected from any creditors if the business fails. This also means if the business is sued, you are not individually liable."

Hewitt added that there is often a tax savings by incorporating, which is another key factor in deciding whether to remain a Sole Proprietor or become an official LLC. "Since we all want individual protection and tax savings, the decision then becomes what type of entity to set up, a corporation or an LLC. There are differences in the way a corporation is taxed versus an LLC. In addition to these benefits, incorporating makes the business a separate entity and does not automatically end with the death of an owner."

A corporation is typically owned and run by shareholders, while an LLC is run by a single-member or small partnership. The majority of people in this industry who decide to make their business more formal opt for the LLC.

There is a fee to create an LLC, and an annual fee for maintaining the company with the state. In addition, Hewitt said,

"... there will be more paperwork, which is not as simple as being a Sole Proprietor. Then you must make some decisions on whether to incorporate as a corporation or an LLC, as it will affect the way the organization is managed and the way that the IRS will tax the corporation. This may require that you consult with an accountant and a lawyer (i.e., more money)."

As with anything, there are exceptions to the protections offered by an LLC. If you are intermingling personal funds with your business funds or are being sued for things like overtime in certain states, the individual is not always protected. It is recommended you check with a lawyer on these and other issues.

One thing that I've learned over the years is that becoming an LLC gives my business a level of legitimacy, eases clients' worries, and shows us as a reliable resource. Yes, registering requires more legal and accounting steps, greater responsibility, and more money

The Perfect Shot

After years of having a clean, organized, and timely invoicing process, I was afforded the opportunity to assist other technicians with their back-office infrastructure. Though I was honored when offered the role, I knew it wasn't something I could manage on my own. The data collection, the following up, and the meticulous way I wanted things wasn't feasible as a solo act. I needed help. As much as I wanted to remain in control and do everything my way, I knew I couldn't. I needed someone's expertise to improve my process and make it more efficient, so I built the right team to handle this additional service.

Building a reliable and trustworthy brand, whether intentional or not, allowed for additional business. With that came expansion opportunities. Be flexible and willing to adjust in order to grow. Being firm and stuck in your ways could enable a pivotal moment to pass you by.

to manage it all, but that's what was in the best interest of my company and the people we were looking to serve. I had to figure all of this out to best provide for and serve my industry.

Bringing on Employees

Moving from a solo act to a full show means having employees. This changes a number of things and will complicate your situation. However, Patrick Murtha says this management decision is often made to help the business handle additional business and in turn earn more money. "If there is a missing component in the business or you are being forced to refuse new work because you are overbooked, then it's probably time to bring on more employees. The benefits are growth, the disadvantage is that you must now act as a manager (in some cases, babysitter), not just as a technician in your field."

Murtha recommends working with a payroll company to be sure that the right amount of taxes are withheld from employee checks and that the money is sent to the government on a timely basis. Outsourcing this service can be very beneficial when you are learning to manage your growth. With more opportunity comes more responsibility and finding the right team to assist your company and employees is critical.

In addition to taxes and payroll, you need to think about benefits for employees. It's not as costly as you might think, but benefits are one of the perks that encourage employees to stay with you. Vacation days, retirement plans, as well as health and/or life insurance, are not necessarily required to be offered, but they sound like a great incentive when onboarding with a company.

There are a number of details and intricacies involved in government compliance regarding these matters, so this is an area where it is highly advised you bring in an expert, like a lawyer or benefits consultant.

These areas obviously aren't my specialty. Because of that, I have relied on the expertise and knowledge of people I trust and who have a good reputation in their respective industries. With them, I have created CLEMCO.HR as a resource for Independent Contractors and business owners. I encourage you to connect with this network's benefit consultant, accountant, lawyer, insurance provider, and other specialists at www.clemcohr.com. Through them, you can gain understanding and find the right people to help manage your business and life.

If you put the right practices into place early on, you can save time and costly mistakes down the road.

FLASHBACK

In 2019, I was traveling abroad with my wife and met someone from Milan. She was very polite and knowledgeable in the area of Forensic Accounting. After working in her field for years, she had a desire to move on. She was bitten by the entrepreneurial bug and wanted to try something new.

We just finished a Segway tour and were discussing the company's business model amongst ourselves. We talked about some of the things we saw, experienced, and how they applied to her idea. We then started talking about what it means to grow and expand an idea into a business. Like me, she was a believer, so I was able to share my thoughts and speak with her in a biblical sense.

I have been very blessed as an Independent Contractor. I had no idea how successful I was until I began to work with and teach other contractors in various markets. Sharing what I've learned with them allowed me to understand the amount of knowledge and experience I possess.

In addition, sharing my blessings with Independent Contractors and educating them to be better allowed for an overflow of additional blessings to be given unto me. That forced me to give more and bring other contractors on board because I couldn't handle the inpouring of opportunity and work. In order to manage the new business and the people helping me maintain my client relationships, I had to hire people to oversee the process.

What seem like layers and layers of systems are actually layers and layers of grace. Through the idea came opportunities, and through the opportunity came the ability to touch people's lives. By providing jobs, income, and knowledge, my company has been able to bless families in a way that helps them project the best image possible for their present day and future selves. Amen!

FADE IN:

INT: FIRST WATCH RESTAURANT, LUTZ, FL. MIDDAY

CLEM is introduced to JESSICA, a health insurance advisor, through a mutual friend. CLEM and his family's insurance has always been covered by his wife's employer, but CLEM wants to see if there are better options available to them.

CLEM and JESSICA choose to meet at a quiet local restaurant because of the convenience it offers CLEM rather than going to JESSICA's office.

                    JESSICA:
    Hi Clem! Over here.

JESSICA waves CLEM to the table where she's already seated. JESSICA makes it a habit to be punctual. She believes in the highest level of service.

                    CLEM:
    Hi. It's so nice to meet you in person.

They previously spoke over the phone about CLEM's situation and his goals for the family, but Jessica wanted to meet in person as well.

> **JESSICA:**
> Likewise! (They shake hands and CLEM sits down at the table) So, I researched some plans and I wanted to show you what I found. Based on you and your wife's health and age, your two kids, their ages, your line of work, and your travel, you currently have one of the best plans available. I wouldn't change a thing.

> **CLEM:**
> Wow! My wife said it was a good plan, but I didn't realize it was *that* good.

> **JESSICA:**
> Yes, it is. There are all types of plans available to companies and individuals, and you have a *really* good one. Your deductible and co-pay are low, and you have a lot of added benefits including chiropractor visits. Your monthly premium is affordable, and you can use your plan in all fifty states. Your wife

picked a great plan for you and your family.

CLEM:
Thank you! That makes me feel better about our situation. (CLEM pauses, a little perplexed) What I'm most surprised about is you aren't trying to sell me something.

CLEM says this not trying to be rude, but understands business is business and JESSICA just gave up her time without reaping any benefit.

JESSICA:
Well, Clem, what I've learned from years of doing this job is that it's about the service and making sure people understand what's going on with their health coverage. I've seen too many people get hurt or sick and then they find out they are underinsured. If they had come to me or had someone care enough to explain things to them before getting hurt or sick, they'd be in a better situation. The proper insurance needs to be in place before something happens. I just

want everyone to be in a better situation and have the right protection.

CLEM is speechless and amazed by JESSICA's response. He appreciates her willingness to help him and others and knows this will become a long-lasting relationship. Due to the nature of CLEM's industry, he knows there are many Independent Contractors without health insurance. CLEM understands that someone like JESSICA will be a great resource for his peers.

1. CLEM and JESSICA choose to meet at a quiet local restaurant because of the convenience it offers CLEM.

2. JESSICA waves CLEM to the table where she's already seated.

3. You currently have one of the best plans available. I wouldn't change a thing.

4. Wow! I didn't realize it was that good.

5. It's about the service and making sure people understand what's going on with their health coverage.

6. He appreciates her willingness to help him and others and knows this will become a long-lasting relationship.

Chapter 7
How Do I Get Insurance?

If there's one thing I've learned after decades in this industry, it's that life happens. You can fall down, get sick, have an accident, have equipment broken or stolen, or even have a subcontractor get hurt on the job. No matter how careful you are, incidents *will* occur. I meet way too many Independent Contractors who think they'll "save" money by not spending it on insurance. Unfortunately, they don't take the time to understand insurance or to see how it's beneficial to their lives and situations. I was one of those Independent Contractors, and I can tell you from firsthand experience that's irresponsible thinking. Things are going to happen, and you could lose everything you worked for in a second if you aren't prepared.

What Kinds of Insurance Do I Need?

There are several types of insurance and each is important for a different reason. From health, dental, and automobile, to general liability, umbrella, and workers' compensation, each plan serves a purpose and offers a level of security. That being said, it's important to find a knowledgeable, trustworthy agent to guide you to find the right plan and purchase the appropriate amount of coverage for your needs.

This is especially important when you are a newly established business owner with a grand idea but a tight budget. I have seen and experienced how properly allocating your finances can make or break you. It is important to make your funds last and save money when and where you can. A way to do this is by bundling you plans. Similar to your cable, phone, and internet, a skilled agent can bundle policies to ensure you are getting the best rates.

Insurance for You:

Start with insurance for yourself—health, life, and disability. The law requires you to insure your car before you drive it; you should have the same thought process about insurance on yourself. You are your business! You are the nuts, bolts, screwdriver and labor behind it all. If you get sick and need to take time off, you'll not only be out of work and lose your earning potential, you'll also have medical bills to pay. Having insurance provides a level of comfort, knowing that you've been paying into a program that will ease the burden of those unexpected expenses. By having this type of coverage, you are setting your business up to continue excelling even when you have to take time off.

I use the word "excelling" in a grander sense of the big picture. If you are working hard and in a nice stride, getting sick or injured can be a setback. Not only from a workflow

How Do I Get Insurance?

perspective, but a financial perspective as well. Having adequate insurance will allow you to see the doctors you need and get the prescriptions necessary to get you back on your feet. If an injury is something you are dealing with, then insurance will help you see the appropriate physicians and receive the most beneficial care and therapy to get you back working.

I had one of my subcontractors break his arm in a non-work related accident. This was a major financial and emotional obstacle to overcome. I was relieved to know he had been introduced to the CLEMCO.HR health insurance service provider, and he had options to receive the necessary surgical and recovery treatment. Without insurance, his life would have taken a major hit. All of his out-of-pocket costs would have been significantly higher, which would have eaten deeper into his financial reserves. In addition, the time it would have taken him to get back to work would have increased because he would have been unable to afford the required procedures,

> **C.L.E.M. Note**
>
> **Don't Forget Life Insurance**
>
> If you die, your business dies with you. That income stops going to your family and the life you built together changes drastically.
>
> If you're young and single, you can start by purchasing just enough life insurance to cover your funeral (about $10-$15,000). This way, your loved ones don't have to incur the cost of your burial.
>
> If you have a wife and kids, life insurance gives your family time to grieve and mourn your loss. If you purchase a plan that is based on your projected earnings, it can also set them up for success in your absence.

medications, and physical therapy. As an Independent Contractor, these factors would have affected his business because without him working, the business doesn't function.

Having the proper guidance is paramount when choosing a health insurance plan. It can be very confusing and feel like a huge undertaking. There are a multitude of providers, options for coverage and deductibles from which to select. The overwhelming feeling often causes analysis paralysis, or the state of over-thinking a situation so a decision is never taken or made. I understood this and wanted to have a conversation with a health advisor. Not only did I want this conversation for myself, but I also wanted it for others as well. Thus, I turned my conversations into interviews on my podcast, The Production Channel. Episodes 21 and 22 are dedicated solely to informing listeners of aspects of health insurance they may not have already known. By having the conversation, and you listening in, my audience members are able to learn from professionals and feel more knowledgeable and comfortable when tackling the task on their own. I encourage you to check out the series at https://production-channel.shoflo.tv/.

After that, I highly recommend you sit down with someone well-versed in the health insurance marketplace before signing up for a plan. They will look at the whole picture and make recommendations based on your situation. Sometimes it's best to have your spouse, partner, or even your kids on a different policy than yours. This could be based on age, pre-existing conditions, working conditions, etc. The health advisor is there to go through the numbers and help you make the right decisions.

Though it isn't talked about as much, disability insurance is just as vital as health insurance when you are an Independent Contractor. It covers you when you are unable to work due to an injury or accident and will pay you a percentage of your earnings during your recovery period. Whether for yourself, employees, or subcontractors, it's certainly something to consider. Disability insurance is a great value-add, because many companies don't offer it.

Understanding the benefits of health and disability insurance, I've referred several contractors to insurance agents and health advisors. I want them to have the same peace of mind I do. I want them to know they will be covered if something ever happens. No matter how young or healthy you are, health insurance is a must. With the passing of the Affordable Care Act and the large number of policies available through the government, everyone can find a plan that works for them.

Insurance for Your Events:

As an Independent Contractor, you should have both general liability and workers' compensation insurance. Similar to other types of coverage, paying into these plans will protect you and your business should something happen. Most companies and venues require these policies to work for, or on, their premises.

According to The Hartford, a US-based insurance company, "General liability insurance helps cover the costs of liability claims made against your business for third party personal injury, third party property damage, and/or advertising injury. For example, if a customer slips and falls at your place of business," or is injured because of work you've done or a service you've provided, "they could make a claim against your company. Did you know that the average cost of a slip and fall claim is $20,000? Without general liability insurance, your company may have to pay all the costs related to settling such a claim from out of your own business and personal assets."

More specifically, general liability insurance is there for the worst-case scenario. Hopefully this never happens but, just in case, it's better to be safe than sorry. Most companies I've worked with require general liability policies cover $1,000,000 per occurrence and $2,000,000 in the aggregate, or total of the damages. If there are other stipulations, that information can be obtained from the organization directly. It's always best to have that conversation upfront, rather than trying to deal with it after a situation has happened.

"Workers' compensation insurance (also known as workman's comp insurance) provides benefits to employees for work-related injuries or illnesses including medical care, wages from lost work time, and more," states The Hartford. This type of assurance eases the mind of business owners in the office and Independent Contractors/Employees operating in the workplace. If someone gets injured on the job, there is a procedure and plan in place to provide a recovery process.

How Do I Get Insurance?

In the state of Florida, you are required to have workers' comp if you have more than four employees (in a non-construction industry). However, in Florida, there are exemptions available for individuals as well. To add to the confusion, credits are available to small companies which are often overlooked by most businesses. In Florida, there is a safety credit, a drug-free workplace credit, and a contractor's credit. The first two are 2% and 5%, while the contractor's credit percentage varies depending on the volume of business. These and other rebates are often based on your state and company/industry classification. This is yet another reason why it is important to use a knowledgeable and trustworthy insurance agent to find plans to fit your needs.

In addition to personnel insurance, you should also look into having policies for your equipment. Whether large or small, your equipment is a valuable part of your service. From laptops and laser levels, to media servers and audio consoles, your equipment helps you/your business earn income. Without it, your company would take a financial hit; thus, it should be protected. There are business owner or commercial package policy options available for the equipment stationed at your facility, like a computer, monitor, or printer. There are also inland marine policies for equipment you would bring to a job site. Examples of these would be lights, cameras, microphones, etc. If you have tools or equipment valued over $2,500, you should consider having a separate insurance policy for those items, as well.

Do an Annual Audit

An annual audit with your insurance agent is essential for making sure you have adequate coverage. He or she will go over your earnings or purchases from the year before, as well as your projected earnings and purchases for the year ahead. Then they will base your coverage needs off those numbers. The Hartford has done my audits for years. When my business was new or growing, my accountant and I reviewed my books quarterly to make sure I had enough coverage. Now that things are more consistent, we have opted for the annual audit, knowing we need to accrue the funds for the yearly payment costs for my plans.

Why is this audit important? Because if you overreport your earnings, you're essentially giving the insurance company an interest-free loan should you pay your premium up front. If you underreport, you owe that bill at the end of the year. You can set the extra premium cost aside, but it's far easier to budget by

> **The Perfect Shot**
>
> I had an item that was kept in my home and was expensive enough to carry its own policy of coverage. One day, while having work done on the house, that item came up missing.
>
> I felt violated and frustrated that someone, working for a trusted company, would enter my home and steal something. However, I was relieved to know that it was covered under my insurance plan. When I purchased the policy, I never thought the item would be stolen or lost, but I purchased the extra insurance rider just in case.
>
> Cashing in the policy was a very simple process. I signed an affidavit stating the item was stolen and the company mailed a check for the appraised value. With the money I received, I was not only able to replace the item, but I was able to purchase an upgrade. In my eyes, that's #Winning!

getting the right coverage from the start. The last thing you want is to be hit with an unexpected bill you are unable to afford at the end of the year.

The best time of year to do an audit is when you have time to devote to it. For me, that's mid- to late-spring. My workload is not as demanding and I have the bandwidth to gather the necessary information and documentation for the caseworker. The audit is often done by the insurance company, but sometimes they hire an outside service to perform the task. The auditor's job is to make sure the policies, which have been rated on the front end based on sales, payroll, and risk exposure, are correct. They build your rate off those numbers, which affects your insurance bill and ultimately your budget. I am aware of my workers' comp rate and percentage; therefore, I can be ready for that expense when it is due. By understanding how it is calculated, I know what is owed. As the quarters progress throughout the year, I can look at my numbers and adjust accordingly.

As important as it is for me to provide the correct number, it's just as important for the insurance carrier to ensure you have the right coverage. If you're a million-dollar company who has to file a claim, but the insurance agent only rated the company on $200,000 of sales exposure, you're paying about a fifth of the premium you should be paying. Because of that miscalculation, the insurance company will take the hit for not doing their due diligence. If the insurance provider feels the miscalculation is not their error, you could owe the money in back payment, or worse, they could drop your coverage.

The whole thing can be confusing if you're not well informed, but that's no reason to avoid purchasing insurance. At CLEMCO.HR, you can find a notable agent who knows what they're doing and who has the patience to walk you through the process. If you come across something in the policy you don't understand, ask questions. That's why the agent is there—to help you navigate and understand your insurance needs. If your current agent only wants you to sign a policy and be done, then they're not the one for you. Your insurance agent should be a partner of your business just as any other professional you bring in to help with your company's needs.

I like to think of insurance as a safeguard. Similar to bumpers on a table for a toddler just learning to walk, your policies should allow you to protect yourself, your family, and your business. With the right amount of coverage and a quality agent at your side, you should be able to keep moving forward and not worry about the *what ifs*.

FLASHBACK

In 2019, I transferred my business insurance policies to another agency. My company was growing, and I needed to be confident I had the right coverage for my team. The previous agency, though helpful, didn't make me feel assured I was providing the best possible care through my plan. The last thing I wanted was for an incident to occur and my policy not protect my workers and their needs.

To begin my search, I reached back out to Jessica Barnhill for a reference. I wanted someone she knew and trusted. Over the years, I had referred several Independent Contractors to Jessica and her health advisor business, and I knew she was taking care of them. In that same regard, I knew Jessica would know someone who could take care of me as well. I felt confident in the service providers and professionals in Jessica's network because of her level of commitment to my friends. I had no doubt she would surround herself with similar people.

In a service-based industry, you want someone who will go the extra mile. Someone who will take the time to know you, understand the fine details, and help connect them to the bigger picture. For me, that someone was Kyle Houck. Kyle, an advisor with a respected firm, sat down, dissected every aspect of my policy, and helped me understand where I was comfortably covered. He also showed me where there was room for improvement. After our two-hour meeting, I felt the switch was the right move to make.

In addition, although I know my coverage is nationally recognized, I wanted someone local I could meet with and ask questions face-to-face. That's a huge value for me. I like human interaction, connecting with people and building a rapport. That's how I build trust. If I can trust you, then I can work with you.

FADE IN:

INT: OMNI GROVE PARK INN, GRAND BALLROOM, ASHEVILLE, NC. DAY

It's 2019 and CLEM is in a ballroom leading a team of Stagehands. They are assisting Clem with the Video Projection aspect of an event he has done for the past three years. This being his fourth year in this venue, CLEM knows the property and some of the struggles that exist. Similar to his life, CLEM knows the struggles he's encountered and willingly shares them in the hope people will learn from his missteps.

The Stagehands listen to CLEM attentively and soak up every word of wisdom he shares.

                    CLEM:
      My reality check was when I
      "retired" from shooting sports. As
      an Independent Contractor, there's
      really no retiring. There's just
      choosing not to take anymore gigs.

CLEM speaks very passionately because this is a subject that's very dear to him.

BOUBA:
So, you used to shoot sports? (The young Stagehand asks very inquisitively)

CLEM:
Yep! And after fifteen years, I just didn't want to do it anymore. My mind and body began to reject the work I once loved.

CLEM reflects on how sore his body felt after shooting a game, and the long nights of driving from Orlando to Tampa.

In fact, I helped to find my replacement. I trained him and made sure he was as passionate about that role and position as I was.

BOUBA:
Wow! That's cool.

CLEM:
Yeah, but when I left, I had nothing to show for it. I had some great memories and memorabilia, but there was no 401K, pension, or retirement plan paying me for the time I invested. Now don't get me wrong.

> I'm not blaming anyone for my lack of knowledge; I just wish I'd known. In fact, someone may have told me. I just didn't know to listen. So, that's why I'm here sharing this with you.

CLEM realizes people are listening to him intently and he decides to bring the conversation full circle.

> Bouba, I just want you all to do better than me. I've come here for three years now and you smile and work hard every time I see you. You've got a good heart. Be smart and prepare for when your mind and body want to stop doing this work. I wasn't prepared my first time around, but you better be sure I will be the next time.

CLEM doesn't want his passion to feel like a lecture, so he cracks a joke, and they keep working.

1. CLEM is in a ballroom, leading a team of stagehands.

2. The stagehands listen to CLEM attentively and soak up every word of wisdom he shares.

3. My reality check was when I "retired" from shooting sports.

4. When I left, I had nothing to show for it.

5. Bouba, I just want you all to do better than me.

6. CLEM doesn't want his passion to feel like a lecture.

Chapter 8

How Do I Plan for My Financial Future?

In my role as a Video Projectionist, I'm constantly anticipating and planning for what's going to happen next. I look at my equipment list, drawings, production scheduling, and pre-planning long before we begin unloading the truck. I enter data in Excel, draw my cable paths, request and hire staff, and execute the client's vision. During the event, I have to be prepared that things might go wrong or a situation might arise that needs my attention. When I covered sporting events, I had a similar sense of awareness. I was constantly on! I had to be ready to move with the athlete, anticipate his/her next move, and anticipate the move of his defensive player and every other player on the court. I also had to think about the ball, the coaches, commentators, the fans in the stands, and even what the other Camera Operators were shooting. It was very stimulating, to say the least.

As an Independent Contractor, you also have to be "on." You have to be able to forecast your own future—the one you want in a week, a month, a year, and after you retire. Most of us have trouble looking that far into the future because we are so busy focusing on today and concentrating on building our current businesses. Knowing the best financial move to make is far more difficult than trying to anticipate where the point guard and ball are going to be.

Go to the Experts

When it comes to making important decisions and setting long-term goals with your money, reach out to a financial advisor. You've worked so hard to earn your money and an advisor's expertise will be a valuable resource to manage your funds. Find someone you can trust; someone you feel has your best interests at heart. It often helps if they are part of a larger entity because they'll have dedicated teams to handle various parts of the transactions. However, I realize some people may prefer a mom-and-pop shop. Either way, choose

> **The Perfect Shot**
>
> I remember when I first met my financial advisor. He lived in my neighborhood and, before I knew what he did, I always felt he was a good guy. Our kids played together, and he constantly tried to introduce me to other good people.
>
> When the topic of investments and planning came up in a conversation, I learned so much about the financial opportunities available to prepare for the rest of my life. If it wasn't for that moment, when my advisor and his brother shared their knowledge with me, I'm not sure where I'd be with my long-term goals.
>
> Through that conversation, I gained a hunger for understanding. This book is a product of that hunger, and hopefully it gives you some food for thought.

an advisor based on your personal needs and what's best for you. It's more important that you trust your advisor enough to give them the freedom to make some of those important investment decisions on your behalf.

Having that outside opinion allows you to take a step back from your life and look at your business through a wide-angle lens. By seeing your company as an entity, and not an extension of yourself, you are seeing the bigger picture. With that perspective and the ability to zoom down to the fine details, your financial planner will help you make more objective decisions about the future.

Neither my mom, my dad, nor my grandparents taught me how to invest my money or what decisions a man should make when thinking about his family's financial future. I was left to find that information and figure it out on my own. On my quest for knowledge and understanding, I realized that people who grow up in a household with someone who lives and breathes finances will innately learn certain principles because of their environment. Thus, when I decided to hire a financial planner for my family, my company, and the contractors under my umbrella, I was pleasantly surprised to learn that our advisor is second-generation in the profession. His father is also a financial planner and has many successful clients.

Not only does our advisor have the support and resources of his father, but he and his brother are both high achieving associates for one of the top investment firms in the country. Because of their father and their generational wisdom, these two brothers have inherent knowledge they may not even realize they possess.

This level-up style of business and generational planning is nothing new. Some of the wealthiest families have been doing this for decades. Now, because of this forward-thinking mindset and the support our advisor receives from his firm, I am confident he has the skills to help us strategize for a successful long-term outcome as well.

Treat Yourself Like an Employee

When you're an Independent Contractor, you don't have the "safety net" of an employer who will match your contributions to your 401k plan. There's no one to incentivize you to stay on with their company and automatically deduct contributions from your paycheck before you see and spend that money. You have to do that for yourself, which means you have to treat yourself like the valued employee you are.

Once you have tucked away six months of an emergency savings and put it into the form of a high-interest yielding mutual fund, it's time to start looking at retirement investments. I suggest a mutual fund, although things may change in the future, because you are able to access your money without penalty. Once you've set up your fund, the easiest plan to start saving for your golden years is with a Roth IRA. This type of account allows you to invest up to $6,000 of your after-tax dollars a year. This means, when you start withdrawing from the account after age sixty-five, the money is tax free. You would have previously paid taxes on the $6,000 prior to investing it; therefore, your dividends, or earned interest, is not subject to the current tax rates. Since rates tend to rise, you're essentially earning more by prepaying the taxes on your gains.

Some may consider investing in a traditional IRA because that reduces the amount of taxes you will paying in that investment year. However, unlike the Roth, you will pay taxes on not only the $6,000 initial investment, but also the money earned when you begin your withdrawals at sixty-five. This may not seem like a big deal now, but when you are older and on a fixed income, every saved dollar counts.

There will come a day when you no longer can, or possibly want to, do the work you've loved. It's hard to believe, but it's true. Even the great artist Michelangelo reached that point. His work on the sculpture Pietà Bandini, housed in the Museo dell'Opera del Duomo, displays his frustrations. It was toward the end of Michelangelo's career, and he was unable to create the way he once did. His technique wasn't the same because he was unable to get his body to recreate the vision he saw in his mind. Because of the dissatisfaction with his work, Michelangelo smashed the piece, and virtually destroyed it. The sculpture was later rebuilt, brought to the museum in Florence, Italy and helps people to understand the complicated journey of a freelance artist. Remember, you too are a Freelance Independent Contractor and your own employer. It is imperative that you are a smart self-employer and plan for the day when your mind and body also reject your work. Trust me, it will come.

Start Early and Maximize

If you start investing when you're young, you can take advantage of the amazing benefits of compounding interest. Albert Einstein once said, "Compound interest is the eighth wonder of the world. He who understands it, earns it; he who doesn't, pays it." As an Independent Contractor, it's up to you to understand that value and how it impacts your future and your money.

In financial planning, there's a concept called the Rule of 72, which gives you an idea of how long it takes to double your money at different fixed rates of return. It's a simple formula—divide 72 by your expected rate of return (1% on a savings account, for instance, versus 5% on a CD or mutual fund) and the number you get is the number of years it will take to double your investment. At 1%, that savings account is going to take another 72 years to double, whereas at 5%, your investment will double after 14.4 years. This is why higher interest investments are a better choice. The earlier you start saving, the more your money can accrue.

"Your biggest asset is time," my financial planner says. The more time you have, the more your money can work for you in the background. When you reach your forties, fifties, or sixties, it takes a considerably larger investment in order to catch up to where you would have been had you started saving in your twenties. If you don't save enough to retire, you may have to keep working long into your sixties and seventies.

A good financial advisor will help direct your investments to meet your needs. If you start saving later in life, you might want to opt for higher-risk/higher-return options. This typically isn't the pattern for someone older, because they tend to be more conservative. Before having the conversation and making any decisions, you should at least know the basics of your retirement savings options.

Roth IRA: These are limited to an annual contribution of $6,000. If you are over fifty, then you are allowed to put up to $7,000 in your Roth as a way to catch up. That $6,000 contribution is just $500 a month, or $125 a week. If you build that expense into your budget from the beginning, you won't have to think about it. The money you put into your Roth is post-tax dollars, so withdrawals after age sixty-five are tax free.

SIMPLE IRA: Savings Incentive Match Plans for Employees (which is what SIMPLE stands for) have higher contribution limits than traditional IRAs (Individual Retirement Accounts). They work the same way, for the most part. You can set up a SIMPLE IRA for yourself and/or any employee who is making more than $5,000 a year with your company. As the employer, you can choose to match the employees' contribution, if you wish. SIMPLE IRAs have a limit of $13,000 per year, with a $3,000 additional contribution allowance for anyone over fifty. These pre-tax investments are taxed when you begin to withdraw from the account at age sixty-five.

> **C.L.E.M. Note**
>
> **Make it Easy on Yourself**
>
> I have the equivalent of $20 per day transferred out of my bank account on a monthly basis. That money is then put into my mutual fund. At the end of the year, $6,000 of that is put into my Roth, and the remaining $1,300 is invested based on my advisor's evaluation of the current market. This is an easy, automatic way for me to save. I hardly notice the withdrawals and my money is always working in the background.

SEP IRA: This Simplified Employee Pension is a little more complicated, despite its name. An employer can contribute up to 25% of an employee's annual income, up to $56,000 to this account, as opposed to the employee making his/her own contributions. This is another tax-deferred account and has more rules and restrictions than a SIMPLE IRA. This is why it's best to talk with a CLEMCO.HR financial planner about the best option.

Other Long-Term Planning Considerations

According to my financial planner, saving for retirement is really all about changing behavior so that the savings become automatic. You can set up automatic withdrawals from your bank account, so you don't even notice the expense. Be sure, as you do with everything else, to keep this budget "bucket" in place whenever you revisit your expenses. Retirement savings shouldn't be an afterthought—it should be part of your everyday planning.

You may want to look at long-term care plans for assisted living/nursing facilities as well. I know it may seem a little early for that, but I like to look at it from a different perspective. There's a new facility being built not far from my home, and as I ride my bike by it from time to time, I think of it as a beautiful resort. I am a traveling technician and I have stayed at many nice hotels. The facilities, food, staff and attention to detail at these properties have often been very comforting while I'm away from home. If I plan accordingly, when I get to that place in life where I need the help, I can stay at the St. Regis of nursing homes.

With that thought, I think I'll take Einstein's advice and let the compounding begin now.

In addition to life insurance, there's also the idea of establishing a trust. This way, when you transition or pass away, the estate doesn't need to go to probate. This can be a long, drawn-out process but is avoidable with the proper planning. These, and so many other, issues can be discussed with and handled by your financial planner. It's important to feel comfortable having these conversations, and it's also best to keep your advisor in the loop regarding your medical conditions. By having a financial advisor with whom I have a rapport and trust, I can stay ahead of the game and best provide for myself and my family.

Beginning to Understand What Retirement Means to Me

I recently moderated a panel discussion at the FAMU-FSU College of Engineering in Tallahassee, Florida. As I sat there, I looked at all the bright, eager, soon-to-be graduates and paused to reflect on how far I had come in my life. I was once homeless, sleeping in a car, and then sleeping on a floor or couch for nearly four years. When I was fortunate enough to become a college student, I had no idea how to get from where I was to where I wanted to be. In fact, I didn't even know where I wanted to be. There was no course or path to help guide my way, and I didn't know how to find it. I just followed my heart and my passion. That was my compass. Now, it is my mission to backtrack my trail, clear away the overgrown foliage, and help others along their personal journey.

FLASHBACK

When I travel for work, I use that as an opportunity to connect with family and friends who live in the area. I was in Houston supporting an event for one of the top social media companies and decided to visit one of my longtime friends, and fraternity brother, Dwayne "Broc" Broxton. He and his family lived outside of the city but close to the airport. It was perfect. I could stay with them after my job was complete and head out the next morning.

They had recently moved into their home, and it was gorgeous. His wife did an excellent job decorating, and it was a perfect environment to raise a family. After the tour and dinner, Broc and I sat around, sipped on cocktails, and began one of our typical cerebral and introspective conversations. I recalled when Broc lived in Tampa and would discuss his retirement, investments, and just overall consciousness about finances. Back then, everything he said was over my head and out of my line of sight. I just didn't get it. My thought process and life didn't allow me to see that far ahead, because I hadn't yet experienced enough in my life or business to understand the importance of his words. Now, I was ready.

After retiring from sports, my whole life changed. My outlook on success was different, and I was now in a place where my brother and I could talk about the next steps.

You may not be in the place to fully comprehend or understand everything that's being said around you. It's okay. It's not your time. *Just be open.* Be open to the information and feel blessed to be in a place to be able to overhear it. Even though I wasn't ready to hear them at the time, I retained all of those things Broc mentioned somewhere in the back of my mind. So, when I finally grasped the concept and met with my financial planner, I had a foundational understanding. I felt ahead of the game and confident with what I knew. Not arrogant as though I knew it all, but aware of the significance of the conversation being had.

Act III:
The Walk-Out

Your mind and body are beginning to reject the work you love.
It's time to think about exiting. Are you prepared?

FADE IN:

INT: WASHINGTON MARRIOTT WARDMAN PARK, MARRIOTT BALLROOM, WASHINGTON, DC. DAY

It's August of 2016 and CLEM has been serving as the primary Video Projectionist for KARI and her clients for several years. CLEM has come a long way since first approaching KARI back in 2011. CLEM still loves his work but the extensive traveling is taking a toll on CLEM's marriage and home life. CLEM finished his fifteen-season career with FOX Sports and the Orlando Magic in April of that year and is now exploring other opportunities. CLEM wants to teach Video Projection, and this thought stays on his mind as he goes to work.

KARI has asked CLEM to travel to D.C. to assist with the load-in for one of her events. CLEM, knowing how much KARI appreciates his work and dedication to a project, happily accepts. CLEM had been working on a Standard Operating Procedure for his skills as a Video Projectionist to include in his workbook and is now collecting photos for his PowerPoint presentation. CLEM realized, after training his replacement for the NBA broadcast, how much information he possesses about his craft and wants to make sure it is available for people coming up in the industry behind him.

CLEM is in the ballroom, directing his Projection Assist, JOHN BREWER, and a team of Stagehands with the tasks that need to be completed. CLEM's style of leadership is from an educational approach because he wants to ensure the local labor understands his needs and can effectively execute them.

> CLEM:
> Hey guys! Let's un-lid these projectors and place them in a row. I would like to look at the lumens to balance my light output.

CLEM tries to delegate in a way that not only gives the task but also explains why the task is important. His goal is to educate and help influence the next generation of Video Projectionists.

> JOHN:
> So, why do we need to do that?

JOHN is happy to assist but is inquisitive.

CLEM can clearly see the wheels turning in JOHN's head.

> CLEM:
> Well, if I average the light output of my projectors, I can maximize the brightness without having one screen brighter than the next. Make sense?

> JOHN:
> Yeah, I get it.

The day goes on, and CLEM is thoroughly enjoying his time working with JOHN. He is hard working, determined, very introspective, and reminds CLEM a lot of himself. JOHN poses for, and takes a few of, CLEM's photos for his Video Projection 101 presentation.

> JOHN:
> So, you're teaching a class on Video Projection?

> CLEM:
> Yes! (CLEM says with excitement and passion) I have so much information that I've learned throughout my life, and I know it will help elevate other people's careers. I have already retired once as an

Independent Contractor, and I know my mortality. I don't want what I've learned to die with me. It may sound morbid, but you can't look at it that way. You have to look at it realistically. We will all transition one day. I just want to make sure I give all I can before I do. To me, that's Projection 101.

JOHN listens intently to CLEM and sees him for the teacher he is. JOHN understands where he wants to take his career and knows CLEM can help guide him there.

JOHN:
Can we keep in touch after this show?

CLEM:
Certainly!

1. KARI has asked CLEM to travel to Washington to assist with the load-in for one of her events.

2. CLEM tries to delegate in a way that not only gives the task, but also explains why the task is important.

3. JOHN is happy to assist but is inquisitive.

4. The day goes on, and CLEM is thoroughly enjoying his time working with JOHN.

5. JOHN listens intently to CLEM and sees him for the teacher he is.

6. JOHN: Can we keep in touch after this show?
CLEM: Certainly!

Chapter 9
How Do I Retire?

At the height of my career, I spent most of my days hopping on planes, sleeping in hotels, and spending weeks at a time in cities all around the country. Virtually every week there were bright lights, scenic sites, music, shows, and fancy clothes that accompanied the corporate events I worked. Although it may sound exciting and adventurous, that wasn't where I needed to be. In fact, it was beginning to become clear to me that it wasn't where I *wanted* to be, either.

I was spreading myself too thin. I needed to make a change because my family needed me, and I needed them. By prioritizing my on-demand career above all, I had been chasing a rabbit I was never going to catch.

I spent too many years trying to maintain two careers, that I was unable to clearly see where I was headed or how my decisions were impacting my personal life. I thought quitting sports would change everything. Instead, the work in corporate events picked up, and I was gone just as much, if not more.

How Do I Maintain a Healthy Balance?

This was a question that haunted me. My family needed me, my business needed me, and I couldn't figure out how to balance the two. In fact, my entire life was imbalanced and had been for as long as I could remember. I grew up as an only child in a single parent household and spent a lot of my time in an environment that fostered and promoted the arts, creativity, and relationship building—all right-brain processes. Structure, discipline and rational traits, left-side processes, weren't as encouraged. Therefore, I never properly developed those skill sets like I should have. I understand my mother did her best. As a single parent trying to manage her own life, find a new career, and raise a child, she had many obstacles to overcome and only so many hours in a day to do it.

During my teenage years, we had our church, family, friends, and counselors who encouraged my mother and I through our situation. Because of their support, and my understanding of the importance of talking through your problems, I had no hesitation seeking professional help when my life became too much to bear. Andrá Ward and Becky Campbell helped me find my deficiencies and the source of my stress. They helped me see why I was having issues at home and how my wife was the balance I needed in my life. Because of Andrá, Becky, and the numerous other people I had as role models, I began to see that my wife completed me. Just as Dorothy Boyd did for Jerry in the movie, *Jerry Maguire,* my wife was the structure and discipline I needed. God brought her into my life to fill my voids.

While working one of my favorite conventions, I learned about the Herrmann Brain Dominance Instrument method of Whole Brain Thinking. I began to see where I was on the spectrum and what I needed. Although I wanted to freely float around the country doing shows, feeling accepted and validated for my work, and experiencing a natural high for what we were able to accomplish as a team, I needed a home base. I needed a place with family, friends, neighbors, activities, and a church. I needed a community my wife and kids were a part of, and one where we could grow as a unit. When I was on the road, I had that feeling with my team, but it didn't exist with my family.

I understand that a wife and kids aren't a part of everyone's balance. Sometimes it's other family members, friends, a church, or a hobby. Whatever it is, you need something that will pull you out of your business. Something that's greater than your trade, greater than your craft, but something that's not just a quick escape. You need something that grounds you. Stepping away helps you refocus your sight and refuel your energy for whatever lies on the journey ahead. I know too many people in my industry who go from job to job to job without a break. That is unhealthy and, most of all, unsustainable. From that imbalance come heightened stress,

> **The Perfect Shot**
>
> I know that I am a creative person who can float around and enjoy life. Going to the gym, however, requires discipline and a routine. I used my desire to stay in shape as a means to create a workout program. In short, I projected my goals and developed a plan to achieve them.
>
> By combining my left and right brain thinking, I was able to establish the CLEMCO.HR Workout Plan. Check it out and give it a try!
>
> www.clemcohr.com

anxiety, short tempers, and an inability to provide your best service. Not to mention, that type of lifestyle damages the relationships left untended while you are away.

I've also seen how an imbalanced life affects one's heath and eating habits. Obesity, diabetes, and other heart conditions can develop and shorten your life expectancy. Worst of all, the stress of being too focused on your business can also impact the health of your relationships. I have witnessed numerous divorces, estranged parent-child relationships, and individual cases of depression among people in my industry. This isn't just about building a 1099 business—it's about building a lifestyle—a *life*.

After I realigned my focus, my family became the refuge I longed for. My entire life I wanted love, affection, and acceptance. What I didn't realize as I spent years looking for those feelings in my work, was that everything I craved was right in front of me. I couldn't see or recognize it because I had been so focused on my creativity and outside relationships that I couldn't see that the structure and discipline that my family provided was the ultimate love. My family's love was the framework that complimented my right brain thinking and built a healthy balance around me.

In addition to spending time with my family, I thoroughly enjoy playing golf. Although people assume I love basketball because I'm 6ft 7in, or 2.0066m, tall, I much more appreciate the patience and beauty of this complicated sport. There's something about the projection aspect and internal drive of golf that sparks my interest and stimulates my mind. Not to mention, spending time on the course is an opportunity for open conversations and is a great way to get to know someone.

We have even taken up golf as a family. My son and daughter both play and we have incorporated the sport into our vacation itineraries. From a long-term perspective, I see this hobby as something I can do well into my latter years, and it can become a generational activity we can all play and enjoy.

When I was a child, I didn't spend time doing things like that with my father or my grandparents. However, now that I have children of my own, I understand the importance of having that common ground. My wife and I have created, and framed out, a lifestyle we both agree on and we both prioritize. We understand this life isn't just for us. Rather, it's for our children and for our children's children.

How Do I Stay Physically Fit?

For too long, my job was my gym. It's sad to say, but it's true. Sitting on the court for two-plus hours with a thirty-pound weight on my shoulder was my workout. It required a lot of core strength and endurance. It even felt like interval training when I sat on the hardwood surface and jumped up as soon as a time out was called, or a quarter ended. After I stopped shooting games, my workout became lifting cases and flipping projectors—another unhealthy regimen. On top of that, by traveling as much as I did, it was difficult maintaining a well-balanced diet and getting the amount of sleep my body required.

I realized I needed to do better and treat myself with more

Career Projection 101

respect. I needed to be in the gym, working out and preparing for my days "in the office." As we all know, we only get one mind and one body, and they will deteriorate if not cared for properly.

I decided to get a personal trainer. I knew I needed structure and discipline, back to the left side of the brain, and a coach could provide that. I wanted someone who understood my lifestyle, my career, and could help me stick to a routine while I traveled. I discovered Henri Risher. Henri is an Audio-Visual Technician who works events and travels just as much as I do. However, he has been disciplined enough to not only establish himself as a well-respected body builder, he has also researched the Health and Fitness Industry enough to become a personal fitness coach.

We've since established a once-a-week training regimen where we meet and he teaches me new exercises and pushes me to go hard. I then take that information, go to my local gym, and continue our routine. If I'm traveling and on the road, I use the CLEMCO.HR Total Body Workout Plan to stay consistent with my schedule. This program is a perfect mixture of exercises that allows me to get in and out of the hotel gym quickly, then down to the ballroom to start my workday.

Working out not only gives me a sense of accomplishment, it also provides the discipline to eat a healthy diet. After pushing myself in the gym and seeing the results, it is very counterproductive to eat just anything without thinking about how it will affect my body and mind. I feel like I owe it to myself to be aware of my health and eating habits. If I'm not, Henri will remind me and make me pay for it later.

What Does Retirement Look Like?

As I got older, I began to think more and more about retirement and what I wanted those years to look like. I had to do a lot of soul searching because I wasn't sure what retirement would be for me. My mom retired from the IRS when I was twelve because she was on a mission to find herself. My dad retired from the military and as a correction officer when he was forty-seven, but quickly became lost without the structure and spent his days trying to occupy his time. My in-laws retired as teachers when my children were born because they wanted the flexibility to play an active role in their grandchildren's lives. But what about me? What did I want? I didn't know.

When I began to define my retirement, I began to think about my expenses and how much I needed both monthly and yearly to pay my bills. I then began to consider the cushion I needed for unexpected expenses. From this, I created a budget using all the skills I had developed running my Independent Contractor business.

Then I started budgeting for the "extras." After adding up all the things I needed to pay for, I began to think about the things I *wanted* to pay for. What do I want to do in my free time? Besides golf, I enjoy concerts and plays, traveling, and taking my family on adventures. I had to create a budget for those things, too. I have my fixed expenses, which will be minimized once we pay off our home and the kids have left for college, and I also have my leisure allocations. By sticking to that budget, I know I will have enough saved for future endeavors.

Career Projection 101

It took me a long time to get to this kind of forecast thinking. Growing up in Miami, the clothes you had, the car you drove, the rims on your ride, the speakers in your trunk—those were the true measures of success. That's how you knew you made it, at least in the world where I grew up. As I matured and learned from the professionals around me, I began to see money and purchases differently. I could look forward to things other than what was in my closet and driveway.

Now, with the money I earn, I can set some aside for savings. My financial planner can invest that money today, allow it to grow, and I can spend it tomorrow. In fifteen or so years, I will have enough money sitting in my portfolio that I will generate S.W.I.S.S. income (Sales While I Sleep Soundly). To me, that's the easiest and most exciting way to earn money.

That's something my friend and mentor, Kevin Carr, taught me. When he retired from the NBA as the Vice President of Social Responsibility and Player Programs, he had a financial plan in place. Thanks to his guidance, and that of so many others, I began to see how retirement from a business perspective could look.

How Do I Know the Right Time to Stop Working?

I'm reminded of the Sean "Puffy/Puff Daddy/Diddy/P. Diddy/Bad Boy" Combs saying, "Can't stop! Won't stop!" That mantra reflects the heart of a grinder, a hustler, a "by any means necessary" type person. I was that person. I am that person. It's hard to see an idea or vision and not want to see it come to fruition, especially when you spend your career building other people's visions and finally have a chance to build your own. When you know it's possible and not that difficult with the right team of people, it's a euphoric feeling.

However, you will eventually need to stop. You will need to rest, and take time to enjoy all you have worked so hard to achieve. I needed to stop, and I needed to rest. My life was passing me by. I allowed things to move so fast, and I was missing out. I had the ability and flexibility to control my schedule, but I didn't know how to stop grinding.

I needed to get over my catch-22 fear that pausing and resting would set me back. My work spoke for itself, I had spent decades building my reputation and brand, and I needed to trust that the right clients and opportunities would continue to come along. The shows will be there, the money will be there, and my budget and financial cushion will support me. More importantly, when the jobs aren't coming in as *I* want them to, I have to accept that God has another plan for me at that time. I just need to be open and listen.

It took a while for me to get there, but I learned there is a comfort in giving up control. There's comfort in letting someone else take the wheel of your finances, budget, retirement strategies, etc., especially when they know where they're going. If they've successfully navigated the path for themselves or others, then guiding you to your oasis should be a walk in the park. I take comfort in knowing that I will be financially set when it's my time to retire. I have found those trusted advisors, and we have made the right decisions to plan for my long-term success.

I also enjoy knowing I've laid the groundwork for those who are coming up in the industry behind me. People like John Brewer, Jonathan Draper, and Johnnie Dazulme can use my outline and infrastructure to be successful in their career and life. My knowledge and understanding is intentionally being passed on to the people and an industry who mean so much to me. I know you all will continue moving forward and, in turn, help others. That's what it's all about. Letting go to let others grow.

How Do I Mentally Prepare for Retirement?

I watched in awe when Mariano Rivera announced his retirement from the New York Yankees at the beginning of the 2012-2013 season. Every team he played that year honored him with a gift and a small ceremony for his nineteen seasons in Major League Baseball. Rivera was well respected and shown so much appreciation for his contributions to his organization and the league overall. On September 26th of 2013, Mariano Rivera's cycle was complete, and it was time for the hero to journey home.

Unlike being fired or laid off, one can see retirement coming and embrace the transition. The summer after my fourteenth season with the Magic, I realized that every game felt more and more like work. I began my internship on September 17th, 2001, but during the summer of 2015, I knew I was done being "Camera 3." Over the years, I'd made so many friends and had so many wonderful memories, but I had checked out mentally. My wife suggested I call it quits and not return the next season, but I knew that wouldn't work for me. I needed to leave on my terms—gracefully. Like Rivera had done a couple of years earlier, I needed to leave with the opportunity to say goodbye and have one last great season.

I felt like I needed to complete one last cycle. I needed to see all of the teams and players that were respected in the NBA and say goodbye. I wanted to see LeBron James and the Cleveland Cavaliers, Steph Curry and the Golden State Warriors, Dwayne Wade and the Miami Heat, Tim Duncan and the San Antonio Spurs, and Dwight Howard and the Houston Rockets. I also wanted to see Monty Williams and the Oklahoma City Thunder. When I was an intern for the Magic, Monty was a player on the team. I respected him then and continued to respect him as the Associate Head Coach for the Thunder. A year after I left the NBA, I saw Monty in the Atlanta airport. I walked right past him as he sat at the gate by himself, but quickly turned around because there was something I had to do. I had to tell Coach Williams that for the fifteen years I watched him play and lead his team, I had grown to admire the man he showed himself to be. I had to tell Coach Williams I considered him a role model and appreciated all he had done. He'd made a difference in my life and I wanted him to know.

My last game was on April 11th, 2016, and we all celebrated as the Orlando Magic defeated the Milwaukee Bucks. It was a great feeling, ending my career with a W. As we wrapped the FOX telecast, the broadcasters said some kind words about me and thanked me for my fifteen years of service. It brought tears to my eyes and showed me that I wasn't prepared for the emotional side of walking off the court one last time. I'm not sure anyone can truly prepare for that final goodbye. I loved my broadcast team, because we gave everything we had to the Orlando Magic organization and the viewers of the NBA telecast. We celebrated the wins and endured the heartaches together. We were a family, and I was going to miss them all.

Through that love, care, and dedication, I had grown in my service and abilities. Now it was time to redirect my focus elsewhere. I needed to build the other sides of my business all while balancing them with much-needed family time.

How Do I Find New Purpose in My Retirement?

Go back to the beginning and look at your *why* for being in this industry. Those answers will guide you in what you do after you leave this field. In order to understand a *new* purpose, you need to understand your purpose from the beginning. Why are you here? To simplify it a bit, why were you there in that moment in time? Prior to your retirement, what purpose did you serve? Don't necessarily look at things from a task perspective, but from a big picture and a granular one at the same time. What impact did you make in your career, what impact did you make in your department, what impact did you make in your position, what impact did you make on an event, and finally what impact did you make on one individual's life?

Marinate on that for a moment, particularly the last one. What impact did you make on one individual's life? One single person. Think about some of the most influential people today and in history. They all have one thing in common. Each had a person, interaction, and/or experience that changed the trajectory of his or her entire life. That moment then sparked another moment, and another, and another, eventually allowing each to reach his or her full potential. That event has been given so many names over time, from the Butterfly or Domino Effect Affect to AllSpark. Either way, it's real.

I look back at my grandfather's immigration to the United States from Trinidad, then to my mother and father's failed relationship, and on to the birth of my two beautiful children to help me understand why I'm sitting here writing this book. My past helps me understand my present, which allows me to create my future. Based on the situations that occurred, my understanding of them, and my reactions to them, I can shape my life and influence the lives of others.

You too have the power to shape life and have been doing it either consciously or subconsciously. In your retirement, you can look back over your life and determine if you are happy with the way you've shaped, or influenced, someone's world and ultimately that person's universe. If not, make that your purpose going forward. It will be far more rewarding than any accolade or paycheck.

I am in the second generation of the Rental and Staging/Corporate Events sector of the Live Events Production Industry. My mentors and teachers are the pioneers who started this rollercoaster of a ride. It's crazy to think we are that young as an industry yet have come so far in such a short amount of time. That being said, if I were to break down the lifespan of the industry thus far, it would be similar to how I've structured the Acts in this book: Act I, The Walk-In; Act II, The Show; and Act III, The Walk-Out. When I was beginning my "Walk-In" to this industry, my predecessors were in their "Show." They were hustling, grinding, and creating a process for on-site success. It was working. Many of them started as full-time employees of Disney or similar hotel operations, and some even became Independent Contractors. All in all, they were getting it done.

What wasn't happening, however, was the establishment of a framework for an individual's long-term, off-site success. The demand and rapid growth of the industry was putting a strain on the Audio-Visual Technicians currently in their "Show" and certain bad habits were being passed along to the young and influential technicians "Walking In." On top of that, no one had yet "Walked Out." The realization of that was a key moment for me. Every other industry has a retirement plan or at least someone who had done it and could lead the way. I couldn't say the same for us.

So, I asked myself, "What should *I* do?" Should I maintain the status quo and continue to struggle? Should I flounder around after my retirement as an Independent Contractor from FOX Sports, the Orlando Magic, and the NBA? No! I got up, reengineered my situation, found the help I needed, and created what's needed for my industry—my people.

That's what this book is—a labor of love designed to help those who are just walking in or those who are standing on the stage of their prospective show. I'm sharing my knowledge and my experiences in the hope that they will help you project your best image possible. If you are that person, if this book connected with you, write to me at CLEMCOHR.com and share your story. One by one, we can pay it forward and make a difference!

FLASH-FORWARD

CLEMCO.HR is a collective of service providers brought together to Coach, Lead, Educate and Mentor Independent Contractors in the areas of Human Resources and long-term success.

Understanding what I needed and could have used when I started my career as an Independent Contractor in 2002, I decided to not only go get it for myself but to also create it for others. That's one of the beautiful things about opportunity. You have the right to take it, but you also have the right to let it pass you by. I choose to take it. Not only for myself, but for you!

#Projection101

C.L.E.M. Note

If you are in need of support in the areas of budgeting, bookkeeping, accounting, financial planning, insurance, or physical and mental health, contact our service providers at www.CLEMCOHR.com.

About CLEMCO.HR

Why I joined CLEMCO.HR

As a health insurance advisor, I support independent contractors and families by researching all health insurance options nationwide. I joined CLEMCO.HR as a service provider because this platform directly connects me with people seeking advice and help. By specializing in self-employed contractors, entrepreneurs and their families, I can offer affordable rates to people who do not have access to employer-sponsored health insurance.

I genuinely care about people and serving them in the best way possible. CLEMCO.HR allows me to do that and creates a personalized human resources department experience for its users. CLEMCO.HR connects you with a team of trusted and vetted service professionals and having conversations with them saves you a considerable amount of time. In addition, CLEMCO.HR makes sure its users have all the benefits a W2 employee has at any large company. The service professionals will educate you on the plans and details that relate to your situation, then they will customize a solution for your needs as an independent contractor. CLEMCO.HR bridges the gap of what an employer does for employees by fostering an environment where you can do it for yourself. The service providers of CLEMCO.HR are meant to serve you throughout your career and over your lifetime.

Jessica Barnhill
CLEMCO.HR Health Insurance Advisor

About CLEMCO.HR

How has CLEMCO.HR helped me?

Clem Harrod, owner of CLEMCO.HR, has taken the time to listen to my dreams and goals. From there, he's helped me shape them in a way that makes them easier to achieve. Clem has motivated me to push past self-limiting beliefs and get over frustrations that I had with myself and others. He's also changed the way I view the world, by telling me to enjoy the process and focus on the little Ws along the way.

Clem says, "Every day is filled with small battles that we have the power to overcome, but sometimes we fall short. It's human to fall short, and that's why we have to focus on the small wins throughout the day. When you take those small Ws and add them all up, they equal a big W and overall success."

Creatives, like myself, often struggle with having too many ideas but not enough action. This is a result of a lack of structure and support to see an idea through. This group of tax experts, insurance advisors, mental health specialists and financial planners will help you plan your career, save for a bright future, and achieve the business goals you've been losing sleep over.

Since joining CLEMCO.HR, I have opened a college fund for my daughter, finally have health insurance, and started saving for retirement. Setting these up was stress-free and maintaining them is easy because it's automatically taken out of my bank account. This was very important to me, as a new parent, because I know that saving early and often is vital when it comes to college and retirement.

I encourage all of my fellow freelancers and entrepreneurs to use CLEMCO.HR as a go-to independent contractor resource for all tax questions, insurance needs, mental health concerns, and financial planning. You will be happy you did.

Kelly Foxen
Foxen Productions

Career Projection 101

About CLEMCO.AV

CLEMCO.AV is a labor consulting and networking resource for Independent Contractors in the Live Event Production Industry. With mixtures of career guidance and individual brand management to payroll, tax, financial and insurance providing services, CLEMCO.AV is here to assist you in your success. By gathering this information and resource professionals, we want to be a one-stop shop for Independent Contractors needing help.

In addition to helping Independent Contractors find the tools they need to have a prosperous career, CLEMCO.AV prides itself on being a collective of highly skilled, motivated, and client-friendly Audio-Visual Technicians. These Certified AV Techs have experience in a variety of in-show environments, can be trusted to put forth their best efforts, and will ensure your show's success. We will work with you to make sure your clients, and their End Clients, are happy.

"Our team understands that not everyone is passionate about what they do. Everyone doesn't feel the connection to the bigger picture, nor do they understand how their small piece plays a role in the project's overall success. At CLEMCO.AV, we do. Allow us to help you project the best image possible."

—Clem

About the Author

Clem Harrod serves as the owner and Chief Projection Officer of CLEMCO.AV, which he established in April of 2016. Clem began studying the art of Television and Event Production in middle school in the early 1990s. After graduating high school, he began working towards his Bachelor of Science in Media Production at Florida State University and was an active member in the College of Communication's professional production group known as Seminole Productions. It was there he learned three key skills: the art of storytelling and seeing things for more than what they appear to be on the surface, the ability to anticipate and predict outcomes through shooting sporting events, and how to stay focused and attentive while working in energetic and entertaining environments.

Upon his graduation from Florida State in 2001, Clem began an internship with the Orlando Magic. There, he established himself as a very talented Sports Videographer and continued shooting NBA, MLB, NHL, NFL, and various other NCAA events for fifteen years. Through his contacts in the broadcast industry, Clem was introduced to, and simultaneously ran a career in, Corporate Event Production. Here, he began as a Stagehand and, through his strong work ethic and friendly personality, quickly worked his way up the ranks to become a very skilled Video Projectionist. With a new career focus, Clem decided to retire from the sports broadcast sector of the industry and devote his time to teaching and growing his own business. Now, CLEMCO.AV partners with many well-known production companies and their Fortune 500 clients to produce events for audiences of up to 15,000 attendees.

After leaving sports, Clem's desire was to understand how to best manage the personal and professional side of the Freelance/Independent Contractor lifestyle. Enlisting the help of various service providers, Clem created a platform of communication and networking that offers a solution that didn't exist when he started his career. With the newly found sense of balance and work life integration, Clem is now able to spend quality time with his family and educate others on the philosophy known as Projection 101.

C.L.E.M. Note

Clem is very passionate about, and has a strong desire to share, his knowledge and understanding of Life Projection and Independent Contractor/Small Business Owner Lifestyle Management. If you would like to arrange for Clem to speak at your next event or have him work with your technicians and teach his methods on Video Projection, contact us at info@clemcoav.com.

Photos

With my wife Joslynne and our children Clemson and Kinley.

I am who I am because of the many people who invested in me and allowed me to shine.

From Bowie to Miami to Tallahassee to Orlando to Tampa, Rockledge to Highland Oaks to Turner Tech to Florida State, Seminole Productions to the Orlando Magic to WESH to WTVT to MTN to Sun Sports to FOX Sports to ESPN to TNT to LMG to TEK to CLEMCO.

Whether you are family, a friend, or a brother of Alpha Phi Alpha Fraternity, Inc., you made a difference.

I wish I could name and post a picture with every one of you. In lieu of that, please accept my sincerest thanks. I appreciate you all.

Career Projection 101

Row 1: One of the few photos together with my father, Linwood Harrod, and mother, Denise Philip. Row 2: Left: Reflecting on the night we slept under the iconic Hollywood, FL WaterTower (photo by Greg Wilson). Right: In front of my middle school, Highland Oaks Middle in Aventura, FL. Row 3: Visiting Television Production students at my high school, William H Turner Technical Arts High School in Miami, FL. Row 4: Left: In front of the scoreboard where I shot FSU football games while in college from 1997-2001. Right: With my Fall '98 line brothers and Dean of Pledges from the Iota Delta Chapter of Alpha Phi Alpha Fraternity, Inc.

Photos

Row 1: Catching up with Rick Price and Jason Dewberry in front of the Orlando Magic arena. Row 2: Orlando Magic/FOX Sports Broadcast crew photo at my last game April 11, 2016. Rows 3 & 4: Spending time and joking around with the Steve Uhlmer.

Career Projection 101

Row 1: Left: With my Video Projection Obi-Wan Kenobi, Phil Licari. Right: Overlapping grids with Steve Campbell. Row 2: Left: Completing a big Microsoft show with Zamir Zeigler and Melvin LeGrand. Right: Backstage with fellow Video Projectionist Michael Swinton. Row 3: Left: At MGM Grand Garden Arena for IBM with Stuart Brown. Right: In the back halls with Audio Engineer Jay Richardson. Row 4: Left: Blake Segall and Aaron Barr let me hold my first on-site workshop on their show. Right: Doing big things with Bob "YouBob" Satmary.

Photos

Row 1: Left: I wouldn't be where I am without Kari Hyatt. Right: Tom Kervitsky and Mike Compton created TEK Productions, a company that others should model themselves after. Row 2: Left: At Front of House with the ever talented Lighting Designer Richard Dunn. Right: Having some laughs with Stage Manager and friend Jeff Sturgis. Row 3: Left: Talking chips and salsa with the one and only Nick Farrell. Right: Building bonds with Ben Standfield and Robert Permenter. Row 4: TEK family photo after one of their annual conventions.

Career Projection 101

Row 1: Working in Orlando with Johnnie Dazulme, Kyle Prince, Omar Colom, Jonathan Draper and John Brewer. Right: Teaching a Video Projection On-Site Practicum Workshop on the University of Miami campus. Row 2: Left: Informing elementary school students about television production opportunities at the Great American Teach-in. Right: Speaking at Full Sail University after recording a Production Channel podcast episode. Row 3: Left: Giving local high school students a Backstage Pass Tour of a corporate event. Right: Speaking to soldiers transitioning out of the military at Fort Campbell, KY. Row 4: Left: Having a coaching session with Independent Contractor Kelly Foxen. Right: Teaching a Pre-Production Workshop at Evolve Media Group in Orlando, FL.

Photos

Row 1: Left: Meeting at First Watch with service provider Jessica Barnhill. Right: Reviewing some numbers with service provider Tom Graff. Row 2: Left: Having a quarterly check-in with service provider Patrick Murtha Right: "Getting swole" with service provider Henri Risher. Row 3: Discussing financial peace with service providers Bobbi Grant and Brian Horvath.

Acknowledgments

❖ To my wife Joslynne and our children CJ and Kinley: Thank you for your patience and understanding as I walked about on my quest to become the man I am today. Because of your love and support, I was able to endure. This journey is complete, and I'm coming home.

❖ To Mom: Your strength to leave what you knew as home, in search of a better life, has been an inspiration. I know to never settle and to keep pushing to become my best self. My happiness lies within my gifts and talents, and I have found them. Thank you for raising me to be the man I am; a model image of my Grandfather Clement. Though we never met in the natural, I feel so connected to him spiritually.

❖ To Pastor Isaiah, Pastor D., Bro. Mike, Dr. Gloria, Richelle and the entire congregation at my home church, Jesus People Ministries in Miami, FL: Thank you. Your vision and understanding encouraged me and enhanced my abilities.

❖ To my Aunt B and Uncle T: When I was a boy searching for guidance and love, you were there. When I needed freedom and to be trusted with responsibility, you were there. You both helped me grow and become a man.

❖ To my Aunt Cynthia and Uncle Stans: When I didn't have a home, you were my refuge. When I needed someone to talk to, you were that ear and provided advice. Your wisdom and

Acknowledgments

compassion helped me make it through some of the toughest times in my life.

- ❖ To my television production teachers, guidance counselors, and numerous faculty and staff members: Thank you! By sharing your knowledge with me, I am now able to share it with others. Your values and principles live on.

- ❖ To Rick Price and Cindy Anderson: Thank you for bringing me to Orlando. My internship with the Magic opened so many doors that I was able to walk through. I am appreciative for the entire organization and my fellow interns.

- ❖ To Steve Uhlmer: Kansas City Chiefs and Jayhawks all day baby! Kick Ass!!

- ❖ To Les, and all of LMG: Thank you for setting a standard and allowing me an opportunity to serve your clients. I've been coast to coast and abroad. I never thought television production could lead to all of this.

- ❖ To the TEK family: You allowed me to refine my craft and provided me with an opportunity to do something a little different. On top of that, you all have supported and encouraged me to be myself. Because of you, Projection 101 was born.

- ❖ To Sean Borowski: You have always been a support and a friend. You have been in my corner and asked for clarification when my actions were misunderstood. Thank you for being the Deacon as I am the Curator.

- ❖ To Nick Snapp: Having the opportunity to be a part of your podcast opened my eyes to who I was and what I had to offer. Thank you for the invitation and the reassurance of my gift.

- ❖ To Stephen Bowles: We birthed The Production Channel together, and it was an inspiration for myself and others. So much came from those conversations, and we reached so many people. The work isn't done. Let's continue on…#Projection101

- ❖ To the CLEMCO.HR service providers: I couldn't have made it to this next phase of my life without your guidance. I know my questions felt like they would never end, but you understood what I was asking and why I wanted to know. Now we're here. Onward and Upward…

- ❖ To Stacey Koston, Shirley Jump and NOW SC Press: Thank you for helping me extract my story and my truth. I pray this book reaches the person it was intended for. Blessings.

- ❖ To 212 and CCS Marketing: Thank you for picking up the ball in the eleventh hour and helping others to see what's in my head. There's so much more to come. We're only getting started.

- ❖ To the Fall 1998 initiates of the Iota Delta Chapter of Alpha Phi Alpha Fraternity, Inc., my Prophytes and my Neophytes:

Acknowledgments

Remember our aims—manly deeds, scholarship and love for all mankind. We are an organization that develops leaders and promotes brotherhood. Let's continue to use one another as support. Iron sharpens iron…

❖ Lastly, to the lady I met in the elevator at the Omni Grove Park Inn in Asheville, NC: You were fascinated by my height and asked how tall I was. I replied 6'7", and you asked if I ever played basketball. When I said no, you responded with, "What a waste."

I never forgot that moment, and I never will. Because I didn't fit your mold or what you expected of someone with my stature, I was deemed a waste and useless. You may not have meant it that way, but as a tall, black male with an athletic build, hearing statements like that all my life, I took it that way.

You were one of many motivations to become a successful entrepreneur and inspire people to be true to themselves.

"Find your own happiness based off your gifts and talents. Once you do that, you will stop working and just flow… #Projection101."

FOLLOW ON SOCIAL

Clem **Harrod**

With Career Projection 101, Clem has created a grid and framework to guide Independent Contractors toward achieving their own long-term goals. You can find more from Clem available at www.ClemHarrod.com.

- 📷 @clemharrod // @clemco.av
- 📘 @clemharrod // @clemco.av
- 🐦 @clemharrod // @clemco_av
- 💼 linkedin.com/in/clemharrod

www.ingramcontent.com/pod-product-compliance
Lightning Source LLC
Chambersburg PA
CBHW061218070526
44584CB00029B/3882